MW01232296

Improve Your Social Skills

The Ultimate Guide to Improve Your Life. Master Your Emotions and Learn Conversational Strategies to Finally Talk to Anyone.

Edward Anderson

Table of Contents

Introduction

Social skills are the abilities we use to convey and interface with one another, both verbally and non-verbally, through signals, body language, and our own appearance.

Individuals are amiable animals, and we have created numerous approaches to impart our messages, considerations, and emotions to others.

What is said is impacted by verbal language and how we use it - manner of speaking, the volume of discourse, and the words we pick - just as by more unpretentious messages, such as non-verbal communication, motions, and other non-verbal specialized strategies.

The way that a few groups are better 'social interactors' than others has prompted itemized examinations concerning the nature and capacity of relational cooperation.

Creating social abilities is tied in with monitoring how we speak with others, the messages we send and how techniques for correspondence can be improved to cause the route we to impart more proficient and successful.

There are particular benefits to having very much evolved social abilities.

1. More and Better Relationships

Identifying admirably with people prompts more connections and, on occasion, companionships.

By building up your social abilities you become more magnetic, an attractive attribute. Individuals are more intrigued by appealing individuals as alluring individuals (or possibly seem, by all accounts, to be) keener.

The vast majority realize you can't progress far in life without solid relational connections. Zeroing in on connections will assist you with finding a new line of work, get advanced and make new companions. Very much sharpened social abilities can expand your happiness and fulfillment and give you a superior perspective.

2. Better Communication

Relating with individuals and having the option to work in huge gatherings normally builds up one's relational abilities.

In light of everything, you can't have staggering social abilities without great relational abilities. Having the option to pass on one's contemplations and thoughts might be the most significant expertise you can create in life.

3. More prominent Efficiency

If you are acceptable with individuals, you can all the more effectively try not to be with individuals you don't care for as much as others.

A few groups fear social connections since they don't wish to invest energy with people who don't have comparative interests and perspectives. It is significantly simpler to go to a gathering at work or a gathering in your own life if you know probably a portion of individuals who will be there.

If you are in a social circumstance and don't have any desire to invest energy with 'John' since you don't care for him or he can't assist you with a specific issue, a decent arrangement of social abilities will permit you to pleasantly pass on that you need to invest time with others at the party.

4. Propelling Career Prospects

Most beneficial positions have a 'group part', and the most worthwhile positions frequently include a lot of time went through cooperating with workers, media and partners.

It is uncommon that an individual can stay confined in their office and still dominate in their work. Most affiliations are looking for individuals with a specific key scope of capacities: the capacity to function admirably in a group and to impact and propel individuals to complete things.

5. Expanded Overall Happiness

Getting along and understanding individuals will assist with opening numerous individual and profession-related entryways.

Having the certainty to begin a discussion at a business-related gathering may prompt a new position offer with a more significant pay. A grin and 'hi' in a social circumstance may prompt a companionship being shaped.

2. Get your Mind Right

What sets the individuals who get incredible things done separated from the individuals who neglect to understand their desire? You may figure intelligence, hunger for hazard, or even inventiveness. Those are, for the most part, reasonable-sounding ideas. However, that is not what science has found.

As indicated by work by spearheading Stanford analyst Carol Deck and others, the best indicator of accomplishment in life is none of these standard suspects- - it's your mentality. The individuals who accomplish incredible things, by and large, accept they can improve and develop as individuals. This is known as a "development outlook." Those who are baffled in their endeavors to understand their fantasies will, in general, accept their capacities and gifts are static, a.k.a. they have a "fixed attitude."

Which is all fine and great, yet brings up one fundamental issue. If up to now you've would in general view your capacities through the crystal of the fixed attitude, is there anything you can do to change? As per a post on Deck's site, totally spreads out strides for retaliating and figuring out how to see your capacities as functions in progress. Here they are in short to kick you off.

1. Consider your mentality a voice

How does an attitude manifest itself? It controls the manners in which you converse with yourself in the security of your own head. Perceiving this reality is the initial step to accomplishing a development mentality. "As you approach a test that voice may say to you 'will be you certain you can do it? Perhaps you don't have the ability' for sure 'if you fall flat - you'll be a disappointment,'" the post clarifies, adding that, "As you hit a misfortune, the voice may say, 'This would have been an easy task if you truly had the ability.'"

Focus on your contemplations and check whether you frequently reveal to yourself anything comparable. If, in this way, you've recognized the fixed mentality at work, sabotaging your potential for progress.

2. Pick development

Since you understand what you're facing, the following stage, as per Deck, is perceiving that you do not stay with the contemplations you presently have. "How you decipher difficulties, misfortunes, and analysis is your decision," the post calls attention to. "You can decipher them in a fixed attitude as signs that your fixed gifts or capacities are inadequate. Or then again, you can decipher them in a development attitude as signs that you need to increase your procedures and exertion, stretch yourself, and expand your capacities."

3. Argue

With regards to that restricting voice in your mind, don't hesitate to be just about as cheeky as you like accordingly. Tell that voice precisely what's going on with how it's outlining circumstances, and effectively reformulate your way to deal with difficulties and misfortunes to mirror a faith in self-improvement.

4. Act

Changing the content in your mind is an enormous advance. However, Dweck's site closes with a healthy update that the general purpose of doing so is to change your contemplations and activities. Try not to mollify yourself with a redesigned inward voice. Get out there and try to do what you're saying others should do to yourself.

5. Add this three-letter word

"We've discovered that placing in specific expressions, as 'not yet' or 'yet,' can truly help understudies' inspiration. So if an understudy says, 'I'm not a numerical individual - yet' or 'I can't do this- - yet,'" she clarifies, "it places their fixed outlook articulation into a development mentality setting of learning over the long haul."

3. Personal Goal Setting

Goals could be used and be useful in two ways. The first is the point at which you essentially plunk down and work out what you'd prefer to accomplish. If nothing else, this explains and guides out the spaces you need to manage. The second is the point at which you focus on dealing with those issues for a specific measure of time, and you set clear objectives to center your endeavors. As I'll clarify in more detail beneath, I figure everybody can profit from the main methodology. The second is generally proper if you have a specific mentality and inspiration.

Figuring out your overall "clarification goals."

Every individual who needs to advance their social circumstance has objectives. Be that as it may, they might not have truly given them a huge load of thought or fleshed them out. When you clarify your objectives, what you do is take vaguer articulations like, "I'm despondent and desolate" and separate them.

You probably definitely understand what your more extensive social objectives are. You might need to make more companions, act less bashful around individuals, have your discussions go all the more easily, or by and large, feel surer. It's OK if your objectives aren't even that specific.

Then, you can think of some mid-level objectives by sorting out the impediments that keep you from showing up at your general objective. You might have the option to do this reasonably effectively, but on the other hand, it's entirely expected to not actually be certain where you're turning out badly. If that is simply the situation, one idea is to teach yourself more. For instance, you probably won't realize why you're experiencing difficulty make companions, yet if you read the site's part on that point, it might turn out to be all clearer.

Another more inside centered thought for sassing out some mid-level objectives is to envision yourself attempting to meet your more extensive objective. Also, recall the occasions you've found a certifiable way to accomplish it. Where are you reaching a stopping point? At what spots would you say you are having fears or skeptical, self-basic considerations? Where are you feeling debilitate and troubled? For instance, if you consider how you need to make more companions, you may unexpectedly begin feeling angry and start pondering how the vast majority are shallow jerks. What's happening there? Is that something you may have to determine?

A list of sub-goals for making companions somebody creates might be:

- "I need to get out more regularly and meet new individuals."
- "I need to turn out to be more sure beginning discussions with individuals I don't have the foggiest idea."
- "I need to show more drive to make arrangements when I coexist with somebody."
- "I need to begin feeling more sure about what I have to bring to the table in a kinship."

You can break those average-sized objectives into much more modest ones. These may be specific assignments you can really go out and do. "I need to take off from the house all the more frequently and meet new individuals" could be part of objectives identified with sorting out what occasions you could join in, how to fit that into your timetable, systems for how to start discussions and to welcome individuals out, and so on.

Alongside objectives that are integrated with a bigger target, you may have things you need to chip away at that are somewhat more secluded. For instance, you might need to begin dressing better, because you by and large figure it will help your motivation. If it bodes well for that objective, you can go through a similar cycle of separating it into more solid things.

Whenever you're done, don't stress if what you've concocted isn't awesome or completely fleshed out. You can generally fill in any holes later as you find out additional. Ideally, the activity actually explained precisely what your issues are and how you need to move toward them.

Defining specific practice goals

I figure everybody can profit by outlining their goals. Notwithstanding, individuals will differ by the way they need to take it from that point. One chance is to put to the side a timeframe to effectively pursue your objectives. For instance, you may choose to dedicate the following three months to turning out to be more open to blending at parties. If you do this, there are sure ways it assists with organizing your objectives, which I'll discuss in a second.

In any case, I believe it's all right if you don't seek after your objectives in a super-proactive, intentional, coordinated way. A few groups adopt a more easygoing strategy. They understand what issues they need to chip away at, yet their reasoning is that they'll make it up as they proceed to get their training in as chances introduce themselves. Not every person has a gigantic need to keep moving about evolving by the same token. While a few groups discover clear objectives to assist them with being engaged and roused, others feel debilitated or constrained by them.

Here are some standard ideas for defining great practice goals:

Make the goals something you have a decent shot of accomplishing in around two to a half-year

You don't need your goals to be something you can envelop with an end of the week. Something to that effect is more proper as a piece in a greater target. Then again, you would prefer not to target something that would all the more reason take you a couple of years to achieve. For instance, if you're as of now truly desolate and detached, you wouldn't have any desire to set an objective like, "I need have a huge load of astounding, lifelong companions and have designed four times each week." Depending on your beginning stage, a more sensible objective for the medium-term may be to begin spending time with two or three individuals on a semi-ordinary premise.

Set goals that are testing however conceivable

You should be needed to propel yourself to hit your objective. If you set an objective that is too simple, you'll simply finish it rapidly and need to think of a harder one at any rate. If you make an objective that is too aspiring, you may feel propelled and excited about it for some time, yet it presumably will not be well before you get baffled and surrender.

Try not to attempt to zero in on an excessive number of things without a moment's delay

Try not to attempt to handle the entirety of your social issues simultaneously. You may feel a discernible franticness and anxiety to get your life altogether, yet these things require some serious energy and can't be rushed along. If you take on an excessive amount of you'll be extended yourself far and may wear out. You also need a specific measure of boldness, resolution, and toughness to handle some fittingly difficult objectives, and if you have a great deal for you to handle, you will not have enough of it to go around. Obviously, saying this doesn't imply that you can't deal with different objectives to a great extent if the chance normally comes up.

Try to make goal concrete and measurable

To put it another way, you should attempt to operationalize the goal, just as any sub-assignments expected of it. This is important because it assists you with concocting specific assignments to rehearse and permits you to keep tabs on your development. A few models:

Mid-range goals

Making companions - Meet two likely new companions and begin investing energy with them at any rate, once like clockwork.

Confronting a fear of large occasions - By the finish of a quarter of a year, have the option to go to a local gathering and stay for in any event two hours.

Feeling less abnormal around individuals - Come up with a 1-10 scale for how awkward and anxious you feel in friendly connections. Over the course of the following three months, record how you felt during specific associations and drop the normal rating down from an 8 to a 4.

Improving discussion abilities - Be ready to have a half-hour discussion with somebody you haven't conversed with much previously, and abstractly rate yourself as feeling sure all through it.

Sub-goals

Making companions - Attend one occasion seven days where there will be an opportunity to meet new individuals.

They are confronting a fear of large occasions - Practice unwinding methods for fifteen minutes consistently.

Feeling less off-kilter around individuals - After certain social connections, assess the contemplations that surfaced during and after it. Address the maladaptive ones.

Improving discussion abilities - Strike up a speedy discussion with three individuals per day.

You may have seen that social goals don't loan themselves as effectively to being made evenhanded and quantifiable, particularly contrasted with something like distance running where you can go, "Inside a half year I need to have the option to bring my 10K race time down to 41 minutes." One justification is a lot of social abilities are abstract. Of the parts of it that are more countable, and still, the numbers don't catch the entire story at the end of the day. Making three new companions isn't superior to two if the connections aren't as satisfying.

So don't obsess about questions like whether you should mean to begin four practice discussions daily versus five. Above I gave a potential discussion abilities goal of conversing with somebody for 30 minutes. It's not as though somebody should consider that objective neglected if they just figured out how to talk to them for 28 minutes. Just think of a type of substantial objective that gives you a harsh guess of where you need to be.

The other explanation relational goals are more diligently operationalizing is that the social world is harder to control. Somebody who takes up a game like bows and arrows can approach accomplishing their destinations under organized, controlled conditions. They can choose to rehearse a specific number of hours for seven days, and the reach and hardware are continually going to be in the place where they left them. Socially, you just have such a lot of impact over whom you meet, or how they'll respond to you, or what sorts of connections you have. This can make it hard to chip away at precise goals when and how you'd prefer to. Over the long haul, you may get what you need, yet in the moment, you're regularly compelled to be adaptable and adjust your destinations.

It's fine if you need to change a goal whenever you've begun on it

At the point when you're defining a goal, it's simply a harsh bouncing off point. When you're effectively pursuing it, you'll likely have to make some course adjustments. Possibly you'll have to change the difficulty level, or you'll understand mostly in that you would really prefer not to make ten new companions, and four is all that could possibly be needed.

I'd exhort against defining generally speaking goals like "I need to be the most mainstream individual on my grounds" or "I need everybody I converse with to leave believing I'm the most amazing individual they've at any point met"

One final idea on creating goals: I believe it's better to improve on strolling before you run. If you're socially abnormal, stress over getting to the degree of Contentedly Average first, and then assess where you need to go from that point. I understand why somebody would set more aggressive dream goals. They feel propelling and energizing. Bashful, unconfident individuals now and again accept their lives would be astounding if they were the Big Man on Campus.

Goals like this have disadvantages. They can make individuals put an excessive amount of focus on themselves. Maybe then making progress toward something more unassuming and practical, they set themselves up to feel like disappointments except if each connection goes impeccably. At the point when they arrive at that happily typical stage, a great deal of in the past off-kilter individuals acknowledge they're totally content with that sort of life, and they don't should be a social hotspot. Truly grand social goals can also be established in frailty. A forlorn, socially awkward individual may feel like they're an all-out failure and accept the lone way they can wash away that stain is if they become unimaginably attractive and well known.

4. Behave Like a Social Person

Being more social is not tied in with satisfying everybody around you. Truly. There's nothing amiss with chilling at home and marathon watching your number one show in the wake of a difficult week.

Putting yourself out there can appear to be unique for everybody. Perhaps for you, it's tied in with hanging with a portion of your nearest buddies or visiting it up with the pizza conveyance fellow.

Here are a few different ways referenced underneath to help you better interface with others and how to turn into a more friendly individual!

Ensure You're Doing It For The Correct Reasons

First of all, there's no correct method to put yourself out there. It's OK if you're not into hitting the club each and every other evening or tolerating every one of those Facebook occasion welcomes.

More than anything, you're under no commitment to satisfy others' assumptions, and this incorporates how you invest your energy.

Focus on your gut response here. While feeling near others has its benefits, it's imperative to go about it on our own terms, and such that feels mentally sustaining to you.

Startup A Conversation

Thus, you're prepared to set out on opening yourself up somewhat more and making new companions. Perhaps you'd prefer to gain proficiency with the mysterious craft of "casual discussion" or how to start up a discussion at the following wedding you're welcome to.

Yet, how the hell do individuals do it?

To start with, realize that the individual close to you presumably feels the similar way you do. As indicated by educator Bernardo Carducci, who ran the Shyness Research Institute at Indiana University Southeast, around 40% of grown-ups and teenagers identify as being modest.

Having a couple of conversation starters on hand can be an incredible method to support your certainty when moving toward others. Fortunately, the vast majority love to discuss themselves, so this is a beautiful idiot-proof beginning stage.

Make sure to share something comparative about yourself, as well, for example, "I'm from Florida, I just moved for the hotter climate, and am cherishing the sea shore up until this point."

Be A Good Listener

We as a whole prefer to feel seen and heard. Truly outstanding and underestimated methods of interfacing with others is by nicely tuning in to what they need to say.

You can rehearse undivided attention by being interested and looking to understand where the other individual is coming from.

Abstain from interfering with them mid-story or talking over them when they answer an inquiry. All things being equal, offer your full focus and authentic interest.

Attempt to ask follow-up inquiries where they feel normal to show that you're listening cautiously to what in particular they're saying.

When tuning in, remember these inquiries:

What's essential to this individual?

What are they excited to share?

What do they esteem?

Give Compliments Freely

When in doubt, say something kind. The perfect words at the perfect time can fill somebody's heart with joy significantly better and also make way for a discussion. Studies show that thusly, we also increment our own life fulfillment.

Telling a collaborator, you are making the most of their introduction or telling somebody how much you like their shirt is an extraordinary method to the interface. Yet, ensure you're true to try not to seem pretentious.

Here are a couple of steps for patting somebody on the back:

Pay regard for what you truly like about an individual, so you'll truly mean what you say.

Don't be self-evident. Notice the little things that make somebody one of a kind, so your words stand out.

Avoid axioms or proclaims. Try not to say exactly the same thing to everybody or praise their actual appearance. All things being equal, center on character characteristics or peculiarities.

Get Involved

If you're prepared to move toward putting yourself out there, consider discovering an interest that is social, for example, chipping in at a not-for-profit. This is also an incredible method of offering in return.

Taking part in exercises you appreciate can help lighten sensations of deficiency when meeting new individuals, particularly if you've recently moved to another local area.

Besides, you definitely know about at any rate one thing you'll share for all intents and purpose with others there, regardless of whether that be a love of cultivating, a weakness for creatures, or energy for social equity.

Host A Monthly Brunch

Welcome loved ones over for an extraordinary supper and set aside the effort to seriously draw in with each other. This is a pleasant method to find a time to get together with loved ones — even only a few groups — in a steady climate where you can chuckle, talk, and think back.

And if you're not actually into informal breakfast, decide on facilitating an easygoing supper gathering, all things being equal. Use it as a chance to associate and practice your conversational abilities.

Pick Up The Phone And Make A Date

If you're to a greater degree a one-on-one individual and not actually into bunch social gatherings, take a stab at calling a companion and finding a time for getting lunch or even video talking.

Even better, welcome them over to your home, so you feel better. Keep in mind: You don't have to make an intricate movement for hanging out and appreciating each other's conversation.

Consider somebody you miss and might want to invest greater quality energy with, then get the telephone and make an arrangement.

Talk With Strangers

There's not at all like becoming more acquainted with people around you to cause you to feel like you're important for a local area. For one, it gives you a feeling of having a place. It also offers you a chance to transform colleagues into closer companions.

Start up an unconstrained discussion with your barista whenever you're requesting your latte, or ask your neighbor how her day is going.

While apparently easygoing, one 2014 examination found that cooperating with a wide organization of individuals consistently adds to your prosperity.

Sign Up For A Class

The first step in gathering new individuals is by presenting yourself to a drawing in climate. Step outside your typical scope of commonality and look into accessible classes that you've been biting the dust to take.

This permits you to expand and practice your social abilities. In this way, take that painting or cooking class and flash a discussion while you trust that class will begin. You'll discover it's regularly simpler to converse with others when you share normal interests.

Make A List Of Your Positive Abilities.

Sadly, we invest such a lot of energy to develop ourselves that we neglect to recognize our achievements, abilities, and benevolence. Converse with individuals you trust to discover what they think your best characteristics are. Then, ask yourself the accompanying inquiries to help kick your rundown off:

What have you done in the previous year that you are pleased with?

What is your proudest achievement ever?

What exceptional gifts do you have?

What do individuals will, in general commend you on?

What positive effect have you made on other people groups' lives?

Stop Comparing Yourself with Others

Part of the motivation behind why individuals battle with weakness is that they think about their own "low" focuses with other people groups' "high" focuses. At the end of the day, they analyze the pessimistic characteristics of their own lives with the positive characteristics of other people groups' lives.

Keep as a primary concern that in secret, everyone encounters agony or experiencing time to time. If you wind up asking why certain individuals appear to be more joyful than you, advise yourself that optimism has little to do with yourself, that happiness has little to do with outer conditions, and everything to do with mentality.

Consider killing or taking a break from online media. Web-based media destinations can repress your will to go out and be social face to face. They also urge you to contrast your day-with day life with the separated and altered high marks of others, which may prompt melancholy.

Smile

Everyone needs to associate with individuals who are glad and amped up for life. Regardless of whether you don't feel cheerful constantly, compel yourself to put a grin all over now and again. Not exclusively will it immediately because you to feel good, it will make others need to associate with you, converse with you, and become more acquainted with you.

Smiling is particularly significant if you are attempting to draw in an individual since it shows that you are a positive individual who merits a meeting.

Smiling may also urge your body to deliver dopamine, endorphins, and serotonin, all of which can help lift your disposition and make it simpler for you to associate with others.

Ask People Questions About Themselves

Let's be honest. Individuals love discussing themselves. And if you need to be more friendly and begin conversing with individuals more, you should show a real interest in individuals by asking how their day is going, how they're feeling, and what they have coming up. This doesn't mean you should pry or be truly meddling about the thing they're doing and pose excessively close to home inquiries. Simply show that you care by requesting that they open up a piece and sit tight for them to make you talk thus.

As individuals react, practice undivided attention with them. Give them your complete consideration, and work on rehashing back key focuses. Showing others, you are focusing when they talk similarly pretty much as significant as posing inquiries.

Be More Liberal

One reason you may not be an additional social individual is on the grounds that you're persuaded that any individual you meet shares nothing practically speaking with you. Possibly you think the individual is excessively inept, or excessively cool, or excessively modest to truly be your companion, however, if you're more liberal and give individuals time to open up to you, and you'll see that you may share more practically speaking than you might suspect.

Don't simply abandon an individual as a likely companion after one all right discussion. Converse with the individual a couple of more occasions to improve read on their character.

Be Genuine

Regardless of whether you are conversing with an old companion or someone you have simply met interestingly, you should consistently show certifiable interest in the discussion. Being completely drawn in not just shows that you are empathetic. It makes for really animating and satisfying communications with others.

Don't attempt to mention to individuals what they need to hear or what you think will make them like you more. Simply act naturally.

Avoid messaging or chatting on the telephone when you are in a discussion, particularly if the topic is significant.

Keep discussions adjusted. Don't continually discuss yourself, since this appears to be narcissistic. Simultaneously, being too tranquil shows that you are uninterested in the discussion.

Have welcoming body language

If you are at a gathering or other get-together, ensure your non-verbal communication says that you need to be drawn nearer. Visually connect with individuals, give them a little wave or a gesture, and look before you rather than at your feet or at the floor. Look cheerful and prepared to converse with others so they are bound to come up to you.

Abstain from folding your arms, glaring, or standing in the corner. These motions send the message that you need to be left alone, and prepare to be blown away. Individuals will let you be.

Set your telephone aside. If you look occupied, individuals will not have any desire to intrude on you. Your non-verbal communication should say that you are prepared to blend.

Offer Invitations

If you're the sort of individual who consistently keeps an eye out for your companions to call without responding, then you are not doing your part. Recollect that your companions don't generally have a clue when you are anticipating that they should call, and they may accept your timidity as lack of engagement in the kinship. If you'd prefer to see someone, then contact them.

Call old companions that you haven't seen in for some time and set up an opportunity to get together.

Throw an evening gathering or other assembling and welcome the entirety of your companions, colleagues, and associates.

Invite a companion to the motion pictures, a ball game, a show, or other movement.

Accept More Invitations Too

If individuals are continually requesting that you hang out, or regardless of whether an intermittent far-fetched individual requests that you hang out, you should begin viewing their solicitations appropriately instead of turning them down. Try not to say that you can't hang out in light of the fact that you're feeling excessively bashful or don't think you'll click with the other individual; all things being equal, think about the wide range of various cool individuals you can meet at the occasion you've been welcome to, regardless of whether it's a gathering, a sleepover, or a book club.

Make a propensity for saying yes multiple times for each one time you say no. This doesn't mean you need to say yes to something that sounds totally horrendous yet tolerating more solicitations to invest energy with your companion shows a certifiable premium in the fellowship and makes you a more amiable and seriously friendly individual. If you reject each greeting, your companion will probably think you are dumping that person and not intense on getting to know one another.

Try Not To Compartmentalize Your Life

Make an effort not to see your "work-life" as being isolated from your "public activity" as being independent of your "everyday life," and so on. While every one of these different parts of your life surely calls for different conduct and implicit rules, the most ideal approach to be more friendly ordinarily is to carry on with your life as a social animal, paying little heed to the climate. At the end of the day, don't save all your associating for parties on the ends of the week.

Look for one-of-a-kind chances to be social. It very well may be pretty much as basic as asking the bank employee how the person is getting along instead of simply gazing at your telephone and staying away from contact. Remember, mingling is expertise and each chance is an opportunity to practice.

Get to know your colleagues or companions if you haven't as of now.

Attend get-togethers with relatives. Despite the fact that this probably won't seem like fun, you'd be surprised to discover that you can make new companions any place you go, as long as you have the correct disposition.

Meet Mutual Friends

Meeting friends of friends is perhaps the simplest approach to meet new individuals. Attempt to see every single individual you meet in your life as an "entryway" or "gateway" into another group of friends.

Consider arranging a gathering and advising the entirety of your friends to bring visitors. As an or more, you definitely realize that you share a few things for all intents and purpose with these individuals since you share a common friend.

If a friend of yours welcomes you to a gathering or a major social occasion where you don't know anyone, acknowledge the greeting. Despite the fact that it may appear to be scary, it is a brilliant chance to meet new individuals.

Focus On Your Social Activity

Regardless of the amount you have going on, if you need to be more friendly, you need to set a goal of spending time with others, at any rate, a couple of times each week. Despite the fact that everybody needs some alone time or goes through an exceptionally unpleasant week, or even a distressing month, once in a while, no one should go fourteen days without associating besides in outrageous conditions.

Reveal to yourself that regardless of how worn out or against social you may feel, you should put yourself out regardless.

Try Not To Control Yourself Constantly

Numerous individuals need liquor or medications to turn out to be more agreeable. Why would that be? Is it true that they are turning out to be different individuals? No! They're essentially killing the square inside their heads that makes them control themselves constantly. Switch off this auto restriction since it's futile. Others are typically less critical than you might suspect. They could truly be mindless in light of the fact that they have their own issues. Essentially appreciate being with individuals, without addressing all that you will say multiple times.

Try meditation. It might sound outlandish for a thoughtful person to accomplish something that is apparently a much more detached movement, yet this truly gets you off of your mind. Simply plunk down, set a clock for 15-minutes, close your eyes and bring moderate breaths into your stomach. As you do this, you'll notice that a ton of random musings will attack your brain – things you most likely haven't contemplated for quite a long time – yet that is alright. Just become aware of those considerations and have a go at allowing them to pass (considering nothing).

Doing this will get your head free from abundance considerations that pervade your psyche mind. This will significantly improve your capacity to be at the time when conversing with others, rather than sifting your contemplations.

Discover a hobby that is social

Discover individuals in your space with comparable interests. Do you play guitar? Possibly you should look at an open mic night or the artist's classifieds. It'll be simpler to expand your group of friends with individuals who share your enthusiasm.

You should think about joining Toastmasters (there's a club in pretty much every city). It's a club of standard individuals who meet up 1-4 times each month to rehearse public talking. The subject of your discourse is absolutely up to you and individuals in the clubs are overall quite pleasant, so if you have anxiety in front of large audiences, you can make certain there will not be any cruel criticism, since everybody's there for a similar explanation. This may be a major advance for some withdrawn people, yet it's unquestionably worth the work!

5. Manage shyness and social anxiety

It is assessed that almost 17 million American grown-ups will meet rules for social uneasiness or social fear sooner or later. The quantity of grown-ups who battle with timidity incredibly surpasses that number.

Luckily, there are some compelling procedures to defeat bashfulness and social nervousness and gain certainty:

Don't tell

There's no convincing motivation to advance your unobtrusiveness. The people who are close to you unquestionably know, and others may never anytime get an opportunity to observe. It's not as clear as you probably may presume.

Keep it light

If others raise your timidity, keep your tone easygoing. If it turns out to be important for a conversation, discuss it cheerfully.

Change your tone

If you become flushed when you're awkward, don't liken it with modesty. Allow it to stand all alone: "I've generally rushed to redden."

Act confidently

Certainty comes through activity, learning, practice, and authority. Recall when you figured out how to ride a bicycle? It was terrifying from the outset, yet after you just let it all out and attempted it, you got it, and felt sure. Social certainty works a similar way.

Feeling restless isn't the issue; staying away from social cooperation is the issue. Take out aversion and you will beat your nervousness.

Avoid the label

Try not to name yourself as self-conscious - or as anything. Leave yourself alone characterized as a remarkable individual, not a solitary quality.

Stop self-undermining

Here and there we truly are the cause all our own problems. Try not to permit your internal pundit to put you down. All things being equal, dissect the force of that voice so you can stop it.

Know your qualities

Make a rundown of all your good characteristics - enroll a friend or relative to help if you need to-and peruse or recount it when you're feeling unreliable. Allow it to remind you the amount you have to bring to the table.

Pick relationships cautiously

Timid individuals will in general have less yet more profound friendships- - which implies your decision of friend or accomplice is much more significant. Give your opportunity to individuals in your life who are responsive, warm, and empowering.

Stay away from menaces and teases

There are consistently a couple of individuals who will be barbarous or snide if it makes for a decent zinger, some who simply have no feeling of what's proper, and some who don't mind whom they hurt. Stay away from these individuals.

Watch carefully

A large portion of us are hardest on ourselves, so make a propensity for noticing others (without overemphasizing it). You may track down that others are experiencing their own manifestations of uncertainty and that you are in good company.

Remember that one awful second doesn't mean an awful day.

Mostly when you invest a great deal of energy inside your own head, as modest individuals will in general do, it's not difficult to contort encounters, to imagine that your modesty demolished a whole occasion - whenever chances are it was certifiably not a serious deal to anybody yet you.

Close down your imagination.

Timid individuals once in a while feel objection or dismissal in any event when it isn't there. People seemingly like you considerably more than you give yourself acknowledgment for.

Gaze it down

Once in a while when you're frightened, the best activity is to deal with it directly. If you're terrified, simply gaze it down and incline toward it.

Name it

Make an affluent of every one of your nerves and stresses. Name them, plan how you will dispose of them, and push ahead.

Experiencing timidity shouldn't keep you from the achievement you are looking for, so attempt these basic instruments and make them work for you- - truth be told, they're acceptable procedures to attempt if you're modest.

Recognize the fear

A typical fear for timid individuals is the fear of others' opinions about them. As far as I might be concerned, my anxiety was the manner in which I talked. It is very well maybe something different, like a worry over your actual highlights or intelligence.

Tom might have handily been apprehensive about how he appeared to me as he presented himself. If he was, it didn't prevent him from connecting with me in the discussion. I realized that to follow his model.

You might be enticed to limit your sentiments or attempt to overlook them. However, the more you attempt, the more the tension develops. The initial step to opportunity is to recognize the fear, as senseless or immaterial as that appears.

At the point when you do, something fascinating will occur; you'll understand that you're probably more worried about your own idiosyncrasies than others are. This will give you the strength and boldness to start moving past them.

Engage

This implies partaking in casual banter in the checkout line and conversing with strangers at bars, stores, games, and the exercise center. Furthermore, approach the people to whom you are pulled insincerely. Converse with them. Request that they dance. Ask them out on dates.

Life is short. Who cares if you get dismissed? You're not expected to like or be enjoyed by every one of them. Take a few risks and put yourself out there to meet new individuals.

Try some new things, even if they make you anxious

Join a club, a games group, or a comedy class. Get another venture, take on a difficult undertaking at work, or become familiar with another expertise. Plan something for escape your usual range of familiarity.

Part of beating bashfulness is tied in with creating trust in a few aspects of your life and not letting tension, fear of disappointment, fear of dismissal, or fear of embarrassment hinder you. By rehearsing new exercises, you face your fear of the obscure and figure out how to handle that tension all the more successfully.

Talk

Begin working on giving discourses or introductions and making wisecracks or stories at each chance. Be more garrulous and expressive in all parts of your life. Regardless of whether you're grinding away, with friends, with strangers, or strolling down the road, you can work on talking all the more straightforwardly. Leave your voice and your thoughts alone heard.

Sure individuals are not distracted with whether everybody will like what they need to say. They express their real thoughts since they need to share, draw in, and associate with others. You can do this as well. Tension and timidity are not motivations to remain calm.

Make yourself powerless

Fear of being judged adds to social tension and timidity. The perfect way to overcome this fear is to make yourself helpless. Work on doing this with individuals you are near and can trust. You may understand the more you do it, the nearer you feel to other people and the more delight and importance you escape those connections. This will prompt expanded trust in yourself and in friendly connections.

Being defenseless requires a readiness to allow others to see the genuine you. Be pleased with what your identity is. Being veritable and helpless is regularly the quality that others will see the value in the most about you.

Practice demonstrating confident body language.

Visually connect when conversing with somebody. Stroll with your head held high. Venture your voice obviously and adequately. Shake hands. Give embraces. Stay in closeness to other people.

Be mindful

Care has been characterized just as awareness. Wake up. Be available to the entirety of your contemplations, emotions, sensations, and recollections at whatever second. There is no essential for your experience that you need to run from, escape, or stay away from. Figure out how to see the value in yourself and your general surroundings, including those "panicky" contemplations and sentiments, and simply notice them without judgment.

Accept embarrassment

Indeed, it's excruciating. No one grows a kick out of the chance to humiliate themselves in broad daylight, yet it will occur.

As a person with speech issues, I've felt staggeringly humiliated due to my discourse on numerous events. I would be streaming along as I talked uniquely to be hit with impeded discourse. A few scenes were awful to the point that I would seem, by all accounts, to be experiencing seizures.

Obviously, this made me careful about talking openly; I was excessively terrified of humiliating myself. In any case, Tom didn't appear to have this issue by any stretch of the imagination. It made me wonder, "Consider the possibility that

I acknowledged the potential for humiliation instead of stow away from it."

The more I opened up myself to conceivably humiliating circumstances, the more fearless and stronger I felt.

This can happen to you if you encounter the biggest fear keeping you away from interfacing with others.

Consider the direst outcome imaginable. Is it a life or demise circumstance? If not, you will recuperate, and you'll be more grounded for it. You'll more effectively enter discussions instead of remaining uninvolved.

Challenge your discernments

We place numerous nonsensical assumptions on ourselves when entering social associations. Some way or another, we accept that social shows require an individual to be exceptionally clever, clever, and engaging in the entirety of their discussions.

I attempted to be every one of these things to all individuals before—and I flopped pitiably on the grounds that I was not acting naturally. I was attempting to be what I thought others needed me to be. Rather than deciding to be familiar or quiet, Tom decided to act naturally.

His amazing model made me ask myself, "Would I hold others to similar absurd standards I was holding myself to?" Probably not.

Do you trust you should be wise, clever, and engaging in the entirety of your social connections? Challenge those insights.

The vast majority can see directly through counterfeit experiences. Simply act naturally. Individuals will see the value in you for what your identity is. And if they don't, you'll probably never see them again (or will not see them for quite a while). Thus, don't stress over it.

Focus on others

As I visited with Tom, I saw the amount he urged me to discuss myself. He assisted me with acknowledging how hyper-zeroed in I was on myself and on what others may (or may not) consider me. To break the spell of self-retention, I expected to zero in on helping other people.

At the point when I ventured outside of my own reality, I could see that others had comparative fears about others' opinion about them. This caused a major shift in my reasoning.

Maybe than battling to reassure myself, I zeroed in on helping other people feel quiet with inviting words and a comforting grin. I figured out how to hear them out mindfully and be truly keen on what they needed to say.

"So if you try to be a decent conversationalist, be a mindful audience. To be intriguing, be intrigued. Pose inquiries that different people will appreciate replying. Urge them to discuss themselves and their achievements."

Start little

Now and again, we feel that to beat our bashfulness, we need to do huge things—like talk before many individuals or start a discussion with each individual we meet.

Tom didn't attempt to deliver long addresses. His sentences were brief and forthright. I started to display his conduct by utilizing less and less difficult words. After some time, I turned out to be more alright with talking at more prominent length.

You can begin to beat timidity by making a move small. If gatherings of at least three appear to be excessively overwhelming, have a go at acquainting yourself with an individual who might be searching for some organization. If visually connecting appears to be too extreme at this moment, give centering a shot another region near their eyes instead of peering down.

You'll start to gain ground, and before you know it, you'll become more sure about bigger group environments.

Practice self-sympathy

Defeating social tension won't be simple, and you'll have times when you'll slip once again into old propensities. My falter has incredibly diminished throughout the long term. If once in a while it returns intensely at whatever point I'm on edge or tired. Or then again here and there it simply happens randomly.

Some of the time I keep away from social circumstances when my certainty is low. At the point when I am enticed to blow up with myself for missing the mark, I recollect how quiet Tom was with himself as he attempted to talk. He didn't blow up. He basically required a moment to recover and attempt once more.

I recollect that I, as well, can turn out to be more kind and patient with myself when my fear of social association returns.

If you're battling with difficulties also, practice self-empathy. Be persistent and kind with yourself on your excursion to opportunity. Try not to be tempted to give in when you're feeling down.

When you are completely present at the time, you will understand that social cooperation is not something you need to keep away from. You will perform better in light of the fact that you are really focusing on the discussion and the signs in your current circumstance. With training, you can consistently consolidate and develop the social abilities that you gain from your general surroundings, eventually causing you to feel more certain.

6. Overcoming Fears and Worries

Overcoming fear is crucial for your success. The future has a place with the daring individuals, not the security searchers. Life is unreasonable as in, the more you look for security, the less of it you have. Yet, the more you look for a promising circumstance, the almost certain you will accomplish the security you want.

Stop Worrying And Develop Courage

One way to quit stressing and get the fortitude to start is to design and get ready completely ahead of time. Set clear goals and targets, then assemble data. Peruse and exploration in your picked field. Work out point-by-point strategies, and then venture out towards mitigating pressure.

The second sort of courage is the boldness to suffer, to continue, to remain at it whenever you have started. Industriousness is a type of "brave tolerance," which is probably the most uncommon mental fortitude. Gutsy tolerance is being able to stand firm after you have started and before you get any input or results from your activities.

Intentionally decide to relate and be around different people who appear to be positive and unafraid of life. Move away from contrary individuals, individuals who are continually calling attention to the motivations to be shaky and reluctant to quit stressing. Control your intriguing climate cautiously, and particularly your human climate, if you wish to turn into the uncommon individual, you can be.

Due to the Law of Expression, a gigantic method to assemble boldness in yourself and quit stressing is to support others at each chance. Advise others to "Pull out all the stops!" and that "You can do it!" The more you empower and support others, the more energized and certain you will feel yourself.

The last kind of fear is stress, and stress is a type of negative goal setting. Stress is a supported type of fear brought about by uncertainty. If you stress sufficiently long and hard enough about something, you will draw in it into your life. The truth and reality of this matter is that the majority of the things that individuals stress over never occur.

Perhaps the most remarkable procedures at any point created to conquering fear, quit stressing, and diminishing pressure is the thing that one of my understudies called the "stress buster." Many individuals have returned to me and said that this basic technique has changed their perspectives from antagonistic to positive and empowered them to be more compelling in their work and their own lives than they had at any point thought conceivable.

4 Steps to Worry Busting And Overcoming Fear

Step one is to characterize the issue or circumstance you are stressing over plainly recorded as a hard copy. The ideal tactic to do this is to take a stack of paper and draw a line from start to finish directly down the center. On the left half of the stack of paper, compose an unmistakable portrayal of your concern, the response to the inquiry, "What precisely am I stressing over?"

Completely 50%, everything being equal, can be settled at this definition stage. In medication, they say that "Precise conclusion is a large portion of the fix." Many of our concerns exist since we have not set aside the effort to plunk down and truly characterize plainly what it is that is troubling us.

Step two is to work out the absolute worst result of the concerned circumstance. The inquiry, "What is the absolute worst thing that can occur because of this issue?" You may lose your cash, lose your relationship, lose your employment, your speculation, your wellbeing, or your glory. Whatever it is, record it.

Steps one and two will rapidly begin soothing pressure that causes stress. We have found that it is protected from confronting the absolute worst result that causes a large portion of the uneasiness and stress related to stress. Whenever you have recorded the absolute worst thing that can occur, you will find that you will gradually quit stressing.

Step three is to take steps to acknowledge the absolute worst result, should it happen. Simply say to yourself, "All things considered, if it happens along these lines, I'll figure out how to live with it." Once you have set out to acknowledge the most noticeably terrible, should it happen, you presently don't have anything to stress over. All the pressure brought about by forswearing, by declining to confront what the most noticeably terrible could be, abruptly vanishes.

Step four is to start promptly to enhance the most noticeably terrible. Having made plans to acknowledge the most noticeably awful, should it happen, presently consider all that you could conceivable do to ensure that the extremely most exceedingly awful doesn't happen. When you quit stressing and have made plans to acknowledge the most exceedingly awful, your psyche will be quiet and clear and fit for inventive ideas. By beating fear, you are currently in a situation to accomplish something productive.

Some Useful Tips To Overcoming Your Fears

Face your fears

Staying away from fears just makes them more frightening. Whatever your fear, if you face it, it should begin to blur. If your alarm one day getting into a lift, for instance, it's ideal to get once again into a lift the following day.

Imagine the worst

Take a stab at imagining the most noticeably terrible thing that can occur – maybe it's freezing and having a coronary failure. Then attempt to think yourself into having a coronary episode. It's simply unrealistic. The fear will flee the more you pursue it.

Breathe through panic

If you begin to get a quicker heartbeat or perspiring palms, the best thing isn't to fight it.

Stay where you are and fundamentally feel free for all without endeavoring to involve yourself. Spot the palm of your hand on your stomach and inhale gradually and profoundly.

The goal is to assist the brain with becoming acclimated to adapting to freeze, which removes the fear of fear.

Look at the evidence

It now and then assists with testing fearful contemplations. For instance, if you're terrified of getting caught in a lift and choking, inquire as to whether you have at any point known about this incident to somebody. Ask yourself what you'll say to a friend who had a comparative fear.

Try not to be perfect

Life is loaded with stress, yet a large number of us feel that our lives should be awesome. Terrible days and misfortunes will consistently occur and recall that life is chaotic.

Picture a glad place

Silence for a minute to close your eyes and imagine a position of security and quiet. It might be a picture of you strolling on a beautiful seashore or cuddled up in bed with the feline close to you, or a cheerful memory from adolescence. Allow the good sentiments to alleviate you until you feel looser.

Return to basics

Heaps of individuals go to liquor or medications to self-treat nervousness. However, this will just exacerbate the situation. Straightforward, regular things like a decent night's rest, a healthy supper, and a walk are frequently the best solutions for uneasiness.

Award yourself

At last, give yourself a treat. At the point when you've settled on that decision, you've feared, for instance, build up your prosperity by getting yourself a back rub, a nation walk, a feast out, a book, a DVD, or what small amount gift fulfills you.

Start Relieving Stress And Take Action

The dominance of defeating fear and the improvement of boldness are fundamental essentials for a cheerful, effective life. You can systematically prepare yourself to where, if one day, when somebody asks you, "What have you generally needed to do yet been hesitant to endeavor?," you will actually want to reply, "Nothing." You will at last arrive at where your fears have decreased so much that they at this point don't assume a significant part in your dynamic. You will dare to set large, testing, energizing goals, and you will have the certainty of realizing that you can accomplish them. You will actually want to confront each circumstance with tranquility and self-affirmation. You won't fear any person or thing. And as your fears wither away and your mental fortitude develops, your latent capacity gets limitless.

7. Building Genuine Relationships & Improving Professional Connections

Do you remember that how easy it was to make friends on the playground?

Somebody would request to alternate on the swings or inquire as to whether they could join the soccer match, and that was fundamentally it—you were closest companions.

Building and keeping an expert organization isn't caring for that by any means.

Remaining associated and creating proficient connections requires some investment, work, and methodology. If you're attempting to improve your expert associations, here are a couple of times for doing so in your present workplace just as on the web.

Improve Your Communication Skills

It will be almost difficult to assemble better proficient connections if your relational abilities are compelling or even nonexistent. Imparting isn't just about conversing with somebody or hearing them when they talk. You both need to understand what the other individual is saying.

Moderate down when you talk, pose inquiries when another person is addressing you, and if you rehash back the thing you hear to guarantee you both are in total agreement. Helpless correspondence is at the essence of numerous working environment issues, including low confidence, expanded pressure, and inability to fulfill time constraints.

Give Respect to Others

This is straight-up there with improving relational abilities.

If there is one thing a great many people can't endure, it's inclination slighted, regardless of whether at home, grinding away, or by the barista at the café.

When attempting to fabricate better connections, consistently make sure to keep the brilliant principle and treat others as you would need to be dealt with. This implies being considerate, utilizing non-hostile language, and regarding individuals' time.

React to Feedback Positively

You can discuss development and improvement however much you need. Yet, if you can't think about input while considering other factors and don't have the foggiest idea of giving others valuable criticism, you will not have the option to advance past where you presently are. Offering input to others makes way fording up more profound compatibility.

Accepting criticism from others is a chance for you to address specific issues that might be preventing your expert turn of events. Criticism is eventually about viewpoint and will assist you with figuring out how to see things from different points.

Be Empathetic

In spite of what it in some cases wants to grow, better proficient connections aren't about continually demonstrating you're superior to other people. Indeed, being sympathetic to other people, particularly the individuals who might be in a place that is subordinate to yours, will go far in solidifying connections.

Rather than feeling egotistical in light of the fact that you improved or knew something somebody didn't utilize the experience as a showing opportunity and an opportunity to help another person.

Observe Others

It very well maybe not difficult to feel desirous of another person's accomplishments, particularly if you've been buckling down on something of your own. However, rather than feeling irritated or envious, praise the individual.

If you get a notification on a stage like LinkedIn that it's a work commemoration or they've gotten some honor, use it as an opportunity to make up for a lost time.

Showing certifiable interest and sending congratulations also makes way for pose inquiries or look for exhortation on the thing they've been doing viably.

Look for Opinions

Individual's love giving out exhortation.

One of the fundamental reasons we network with individuals is to exploit their experience, abilities, or information sooner or later on schedule, regardless of whether it's simply perusing articles they post.

You shouldn't email shoot everybody on your contact list routinely (or you'll end up losing contacts left and right). In any case, don't spare a moment to connect if you have a genuine requirement for their assessment or exhortation. Make certain to ask about them, as well, and consistently be considerate and close with a thank you.

Get Coffee

Suppose you're attempting to fabricate all the more an affinity with an expert contact, attempt to take it off the page. Propose a meeting for an espresso and set a specific time so they realize you're not anticipating visiting their ear off for two hours on a Sunday morning. If you travel a great deal for work, put forth a valiant effort to get a cup of joe with associations in different urban communities while you're there.

Check-In

You may not generally have something specific at the top of the priority list to discuss or get some information about. That is fine. You can generally drop a note to registration. This functions admirably with individuals you've momentarily met or conversed with on more than one occasion don't have a setup relationship yet. Keep it short and direct and thank them for their time.

Do Some Housekeeping

Try not to stress, if you don't perceive an association, you're in good company. Put to the side some time, perhaps once per month to perform association housekeeping. You don't need to go through your whole rundown, particularly if you have many associations, yet go through a segment and once again introduce yourself to those you don't have a clue or don't recall. Simply recollect it's also essential to offer your contacts a reprieve. If you connect with an inquiry and they don't react, don't follow up by proposing espresso.

Alternately, if you get together for espresso, send them a "thank you" note; however, fight the temptation to propose transforming it into something standard.

Meeting New People

When it comes to money, work, or physical exercise, it's really easy to set goals and accomplish them. Yet, with regards to meeting and making friends, it's not all that straightforward. You can't simply say "my goal is to be friends with this and that" or "I intend to make 10 friends in the following 90 days"; it simply doesn't feel exceptionally regular or instinctive.

Here are the systems to improve your social abilities, meet new individuals, make friends, and assemble a compensating group of friends.

Why Most Socializing Advice Doesn't Work, And What To Do About It

Most mingling counsel doesn't work, since it centers around strategy rather than a lifestyle change. I do, indeed, show numerous social abilities and strategies that work extraordinary all alone; however, if you don't make them part of your lifestyle, you will not take advantage of them.

Change can be hard since, in such a case that you need to make sure to accomplish something, you presumably will not do it for extremely long. If meeting individuals take a lot of your resolution, you just will not probably do a lot of it. This is the reason I needed to concoct simpler approaches to meet new individuals and make friends. I made a bunch of propensities that essentially mix with different aspects of my life.

Here, we are imparting to you 3 of the best propensities for making friends and building groups of friends.

Go To Monthly Events To Meet New People

These days, if you're not continually making new friends, you're really losing a few. Individuals are continually moving, evolving occupations, evolving interests, and getting into connections, which frequently cause them to vanish from your life. You in this way need to keep up by continually making new friends.

Perhaps the ideal approach to meeting new individuals is discovering nearby networks or clubs where individuals get together routinely. Search for gatherings and clubs dependent on a business territory, a game, a diversion, a social reason, a singles club, or simply broad systems administration.

Go to a portion of their gatherings to see which ones are generally fascinating to you. From that point onward, begin going to their occasions at any rate once every month, if not more. However, don't cause this something you to do when you "have time." Add a suggestion to your schedule and think of it as a non-negotiable piece of your life.

If you need to make this "stick" far and away superior, have a go at joining the getting sorted out a group of that local area. When you become a contributing part, it's a lot simpler to adhere to the propensity for joining in. Individuals will also incline toward you to become acquainted with you better. It'll place you in an incredible spot for associating with new and previous individuals.

Simply this strategy alone can help your public activity to levels you could just dream of previously.

Require A Hour A Week To Reach Out To People

Right now, change is tied in with requiring 60 minutes, week by week, to meet up with new and existing friends. Utilize one hour to do nothing else except for contact individuals—by telephone, text or Facebook.

This is significant in light of the fact that your friendships debilitate if you don't in any event occasionally support them. It's also significant on the grounds that you need to circle back to the new individuals you meet; in any case, those friendships won't ever be made.

The test here is that we get occupied in our bustling lives and neglect to contact individuals, possibly to think twice about it subsequently when we do have the opportunity to mingle however nobody to call since we've overlooked everybody for such a long time.

The arrangement is to ritualize it: Make it week after week calendared hour to get in contact with individuals that make a difference to you. I like to do this on Tuesday evening, yet you can pick when you don't have whatever else to do and commit that booked hour to connect.

At the point when it's an ideal opportunity to do it, ask yourself inquiries like "Who should I contact?", "Who would I like to meet in the coming days?", and "Who did I meet as of late that I need to advance the relationship with?" Your nature will help you to remember individuals you should contact.

Go Out Weekly

As you begin meeting more individuals, set a period inside your week that would be ideal for meeting with them. It's vital that you don't simply do this sometimes or exactly when you recall. All things being equal, make it a propensity. To help, furnish yourself with a week after week update.

If you've set out your week-by-week "connecting hour" on Tuesday, put an update on Thursday to design a social action for Friday or Saturday, and recommend it to individuals through messages, calls, or email.

Try not to stand until you need to go out to propose that individuals accompany you; do it a couple of days ahead of time. As you become more acquainted with them better, you can propose plans with more limited notification. For instance, dearest companions that live in a similar city can call one another and make arrangements to meet in the next hour.

<u>Making Friends</u>

If you followed the counsel in the Meeting People area, you may have effectively made a couple of associations. Perhaps you've looked at a couple of gatherings of people or made a couple of ordinary associations and found some friendly people.

Shockingly, friendly people are not equivalent to people who are your friends. It's ideal to feel invited when you go to a gathering meeting. However, it's considerably more important to have connections that flourish outside of the gatherings.

In any case, how would you construct those connections? It's one thing to meet somebody that you coexist with. It's something else to develop your relationship with that individual to where you feel great welcoming them over to hang out. In some cases, connections will become rapidly all alone; however, if they don't, how would you urge them to develop?

Luckily, similar to each and every point in these friendly abilities manage, making friends is an expertise that you can create. With the correct direction, you'll see it as simple to make enduring, satisfying friendships. This part was composed to show you how.

Making Friends contains three exercises.

Finding Good Friends

It's feasible to be friends with anyone. If a few groups are simply preferable friend material over others. In this section, I will show you how to identify individuals who are destined to treat you well, and whose friendship you will most appreciate.

Starting A Friendship

Whenever you've met somebody that you need to be friends with, how would you get the relationship going? In this segment, I disclose how to give a greeting that will make way for another friend.

Deepening A New Friendship

At the point when you've quite recently made another friend, support that friendship. This part will show you how you can grow another friendship into a solid, enduring relationship. It also contains guidance for being an old buddy to other people.

How To Support Your Friends When They Need You

Well, there's no foolproof formula for moment achievement. In any case, some strong standards and techniques can manage you.

They will not guide you precisely on the grounds that every circumstance is different, yet they'll put you destined for success.

Listen and Don't Panic

The initial step to being alright is discussing how you feel, and your friend will require somebody to tune in to when they're prepared to open up. You don't have to attempt to "fix" their issues, just let them realize that you give it a second thought, and that their emotions are significant, heard and substantial. Recollect that they need a quiet air to converse with you, panic don't as well!

Don't Judge Them or Their Problems

It's so significant not to pass judgment on one another. The fear of judgment can be a major impediment for somebody attempting to approach about how they feel, which means their sentiments and stresses could go unheard. Tell them that you support them and that you understand.

Be There for Each Other - You're Not Alone

Ensure that your friend realizes that they are in good company and don't need to manage this alone. It's significant that they understand that there will be individuals (like yourself!) that will be there to help them at all times. Promise them that everybody feels on edge now and again yet they can traverse it and advise them that they've endured each terrible day up until now, so they move beyond this one as well.

Be Honest

If you're stressed over your friend, disclose for what reason to them in a clear manner. Inquire as to whether they've addressed any other person about how they're feeling. If you think they need it or are uncertain, you could recommend that they search for additional assistance and backing.

Talk to a Trusted Adult

Inquire as to whether there are any grown-ups, they believe that they figure they could converse with, and urge them to address them about how they are feeling. Recommend individuals like relatives, educators, and youth laborers, as these believed grown-ups could possibly offer more help than you, yourself can. Tell your friend that this will not be pretty much as overwhelming as they may suspect and that you're there to assist them with getting the assistance they need.

Talk to a Trusted Adult

If your friend feels too awkward conversing with a grown-up that they know, or only for additional help, you could urge them to telephone to a helpline. There are bunches of free helplines to tune in to your concerns and permit you to talk about your difficult emotions. A portion of these are 24 hours every day and some are pointed specifically at youngsters. You might need to recommend Samaritans, Childline, Breathing Space helpline or any others that you are aware of. Childline also offers online visit rooms with guides if you would prefer not to talk via telephone, just as message sheets where you can get counsel from other youngsters.

Help Your Friend make him feel Better

Urge your friend to do the things that will cause them to feel much improved, and help them to remember the significance of self-care. Ensure that they are as yet eating, dozing and remaining hydrated, and energize other supportive things, for example, removing time from online media and recording how they feel. Accomplish something with them like take a walk, watch a film, or play a game to help take their brain of things.

Visit a Doctor or Health Worker

Some of the time your friend's concerns might be overpowering them to the point that you can't help them enough without anyone else, and they should address a specialist to get proficient help. Assist your friend with making an arrangement, and advise them that the specialist can help them, and that it's smarter to connect for that help now before things deteriorate.

Get Advice Online

The web has heaps of sites and youth discussions intended to help youngsters going through difficult occasions, like Young Minds, Young Scot, Childline and Papyrus. Be cautious with what locales you're utilizing or recommending to your friend, and ensure they're protected and solid like the ones above.

Don't Keep it a Secret

If you're stressed that your friend may hurt themselves or discuss self-destruction, you can't stay quiet about it. Urge them to shout out about it themselves, yet if they don't, you need to discover the harmony between their security and protecting them. It very well may be difficult to do this when you realize that they might be angry from the start if you tell somebody, however you need to advise yourself that they will also be protected and alive, and that they came to you in light of the fact that the needed assistance and backing.

Avoid Drugs and Alcohol

While it might be captivating to go to alcohol or meds when you're feeling low, it's essential to remind your friend that these will simply exacerbate things as a rule.

Distract Them

Invest energy with your friend and help divert them based on what's disturbing them. In any case, ensure you give them space if they need it, and ensure they know you're still there to listen at whatever point they need it.

Know That It Gets Better

Regardless of how terrible things get, they will improve, ensure your friend realizes that they can get past it, and they approach all the assistance they need to do that. There are such countless individuals that have endured their difficulties and battles; ensure your friend knows they're sufficiently able to do it as well.

Lean away from banalities

Sayings like "Everything occurs for an explanation" aren't useful when you're attempting to comfort a friend. Turning to platitudes can cause it to sympathize with like you're limiting the friend's torment.

And avoid insights. For instance, if a friend discovered their mate is cheating, possibly don't attempt to cause them to feel less alone by sharing that half of the relationships end in separate.

Feel with your best friend the bigness of what they're going through. "Recall that since it happens to many individuals doesn't mean it's any less obliterating."

Make an effort not to "foist" or "worry."

Fosters will in general push their recommendation — to demand to fix or defeating the issue. Fretters are so stressed over their friend's difficulties that they are distracted with whether they are doing what's necessary to help.

Try to hold those practices under control, Miller says. "Nobody should need to oversee you when they're going through a misfortune."

Showing up is certainly not a one-time thing

Commemorations of difficult dates can be intense. And anguish is so convoluted and appears to be unique for every individual. Recollect that your friend may change through a few phases of distress, dissatisfaction, or anger. Stay in contact with them and check whether their requirements change. "It implies a ton to realize that your friend knows and contemplating you," says Miller.

Tips on supporting a friend

Realizing how to help a friend who's going through a difficult time can be hard. You probably won't realize what to do, or stress that you're not doing what's needed, however you're doubtlessly doing what you can. Here are some things you could attempt:

Figure out how to talk – it can assist with discovering some place calm where you're not going to be hindered or caught by others. You can look at our ice breakers for certain thoughts on the best way to begin the discussion.

Hear them out – simply listening can have a gigantic effect to how somebody feels. If they think that its difficult to talk, let them know you're there when they're prepared.

Comfort them – there is certifiably not an off-base comment. In any case, you could attempt 'you will not generally feel like this' or 'you're in good company in this – there's part of individuals who care about you'.

Ask them what might help – it could simply be being there for them, or they may need assistance conversing with a grown-up or searching for help choices.

Urge them to discover support - like conversing with a confided in grown-up like a parent, instructor, specialist or another person they trust. You could significantly offer to go with them to converse with them. For additional thoughts on where to discover support, see our page on discovering support.

Do the same things you both enjoy together – here and there doing the ordinary things you do together like taking a walk or watching a film can have a major effect on how they're feeling.

Stay in touch – ask them how they're doing, continue to welcome them to participate, and continue to send an intermittent message just to check in, regardless of whether they don't answer.

Accomplish something nice– like simply making an impression on making them grin or giggle or arranging something little for them to anticipate, similar to a sleepover or an outing to the film.

Be patient – your friendship may feel different for some time, yet there will in any case be happy occasions and they will be happy if you can stay by them.

If your companion has opened up and it really feels a lot for you to handle, that is alright. You can thank them for conversing with you, yet clarify how you're feeling. If you're ready to, offer to help them discover more help on our site. And remember to care for yourself as well.

8. Improve Your Self Esteem

Self-esteem is the manner by which you feel about yourself or the assessment you have about yourself. Everybody has times when they feel somewhat low or think that it's difficult to put stock in themselves. Nonetheless, this can prompt issues, including emotional well-being issues like despondency or apprehension if this turns into a drawn-out circumstance. A portion of the side effects of low self-regard can also be an indication of these issues.

Self-esteem is frequently the result of a lifetime of encounters, and especially what befell us as youngsters. Notwithstanding, it is feasible to improve your self-regard at whatever stage in life. This page gives more data about self-esteem and a few moves that you can make to improve it.

Understanding Self-Esteem

A few groups consider self-esteem their inward voice (or self-discourse) – the voice that reveals to you whether you are sufficient to do or accomplish something.

Self-esteem is really about how we admire ourselves and our insights about our identity and what we can do.

Self-Esteem Is Not About Ability

Self-esteem is usually not related to either your own capacity or others' impression of you.

It is very attainable for somebody who is acceptable at something to have helpless self-regard. Then again, somebody who battles with a specific errand may by and large has great self-regard.

People with great self-esteem by and large feel good about themselves and about life. This makes them significantly stronger and better ready to adapt to life's high points and low points.

Those with helpless self-esteem, notwithstanding, are frequently substantially more condemning of themselves. They think that it's harder to ricochet back from difficulties and mishaps. This may lead them to stay away from difficult circumstances. That can notwithstanding, really decline their self-regard even further, on the grounds that they feel much more dreadful about themselves subsequently.

An absence of self-esteem can along these lines impact how individuals act, also what they accomplish in their lives.

You may think that it's intriguing to peruse our page The Importance of Mindset for additional about what disposition means for conduct.

Why Do People Experience Low Self-Esteem?

There are many reasons that why someone may have low self-esteem. In any case, it regularly begins in youth, maybe with an inclination that you couldn't satisfy hopes. It can also be the aftereffect of grown-up encounters like a difficult relationship, either close to home or at work.

Improving Your Self-Esteem

There are plentiful ways by which you can recover your self-esteem.

Recognize and Challenge Your Negative Beliefs

The initial footstep is to recognize and then test, your negative convictions about yourself.

Notice your considerations about yourself. For instance, you may end up reasoning 'I'm not smart enough to do that' or 'I have no friends'. At the point when you do, search for proof that negates those assertions. Record both explanation and proof, and continue to glance back at it to advise yourself that your negative convictions about yourself are false.

Identify the Positive about Yourself

It is also a smart thought to record positive things about yourself, for example, being accepted at a game, or pleasant things that individuals have said about you. When you begin to feel low, glance back at these things, and advise yourself that there is a lot of good about you.

All in all, positive interior discourse is a major piece of improving your self-esteem.

If you discover yourself making statements like 'I'm not adequate' or 'I'm a disappointment', you can begin to make something happen by saying 'I can beat this' and 'I can turn out to be more sure by review myself in a more sure manner'.

In any case you will discover yourself falling once more into old negative propensities, however with standard exertion you can begin to feel better and assemble your self-esteem too.

Fabricate Positive Relationships—and Avoid Negative Ones

You will presumably find that certain individuals—and certain connections—cause you to feel better compared to other people.

If there are individuals who cause you to feel awful about yourself, attempt to keep away from them.

Fabricate associations with individuals who cause you to have a positive outlook on yourself and stay away from the connections that drag you down.

Offer Yourself a Reprieve

You don't need to be ideal the entire day. You don't need to have a positive outlook on yourself constantly.

Self-esteem changes from one circumstance to another, from one day to another and hour to hour. A few groups feel loose and good with friends and partners, yet uncomfortable and modest with strangers. Others may feel absolutely in command of themselves at work yet battle socially (or the other way around).

Offer yourself a reprieve. We as an entire have times when we feel a clenched down or think that its harder to keep up our self-conviction.

The key isn't to be too hard on yourself. Be caring to yourself, and not very basic.

Try not to condemn yourself to other people, since this can build up your antagonistic perspectives and give others a (perhaps bogus) adverse assessment of you.

You can assist with boosting your self-esteem by giving yourself a treat at whatever point you prevail with regards to accomplishing something hard, or only for dealing with an especially awful day.

Get clear on your qualities.

Figure out what your qualities are and analyze your life to see where you're not living in arrangement with what you accept. Then roll out any important improvements. The more you understand a big motivator for you, the more sure you will be.

Challenge your limiting convictions.

At the point when you discover yourself pondering yourself, pause and challenge yourself. Try not to leave yourself alone restricted by mistaken convictions.

Stand at the corner of your usual range of familiarity

Expand yourself and move to the edge of your usual range of familiarity. Get awkward - have a go at something new, meet different individuals or whimsically approach a circumstance. Certainty starts at the edge of your usual range of familiarity.

Help someone.

Use your gifts, capacities, and abilities to help others. Give someone direct assistance, share strong resources, or empower someone with something they need to learn. Offer something you do well as a gift to someone.

Mend your past

Uncertain issues and dramatization can keep you caught in low self-esteem. Look for the help of a prepared guide to assist you with recuperating the past so you could migrate onto the future in a certain and self-insured way.

Quit stressing over others' opinions

When you stress over others' opinions about you, you don't hesitate to be totally yourself. Settle on a firm choice to quit stressing over other's opinions - start settling on decisions dependent on what you need, not what you think others need from you.

Peruse something helpful

An incredible method to acquire self-esteem is to peruse something that lifts you up and causes you to feel good about yourself.

Recover your respectability

Characterize how trustworthiness affects you, and guarantee that you're living as per that understanding. If your life isn't lined up with your character, it will deplete you and leave you feeling terrible about yourself.

Let Bad and negative People Go

If there are persons in your life who are negative- - who have nothing sure to say or who put you down or exploit you- - do the shrewd thing and let them go. The best way to track down your self-esteem is to encircle yourself with steady sure individuals who appreciate you and worth you.

Attract a line to the sand

The ideal approach to track down your self-esteem is to make individual limits. Understand what your limits are and how you wish to react when individuals cross them. Try not to permit others to control you, exploit you or control you. To be sure is to keep up firm limits.

Care about your appearance

At the point when you put your best self forward, you feel your best. Dress like somebody who has certainty and allowed your self-affirmation to come through by the way you look.

Welcome disappointment as a component of development

It's a typical reaction to be challenging for yourself when you've fizzled. In any case, if you can shift your deduction to understand that disappointment is a chance to realize, that it assumes a fundamental part in learning and development, it can help you keep viewpoint. Recollect too that disappointment implies you're putting forth an attempt.

Continuously stay an understudy

Consider yourself a lifelong student. Approach all that you do with an understudy's attitude - what Zen Buddhists call Shoshin or "amateur's brain"- - open, excited, fair-minded, and willing to learn.

Become More Positive and use to Say No

Individuals with low self-esteem frequently think that it's difficult to stand up for themselves or deny others.

This implies that they may get over-troubled at home or at work since they don't care to decline anybody anything. Nonetheless, this can expand pressure and make it much harder to oversee.

Building up your decisiveness can thusly assist with improving your self-esteem. Some of the time going about as though you put stock in yourself can really assist with expanding self-conviction!

Improve Your Physical Health

It is a lot simpler to have a positive outlook on ourselves when we are fit and healthy. In any case, individuals with low self-esteem frequently disregard themselves, since they don't feel that they 'have the right to be taken care of.

Take a stab at taking more exercise, eating great, and getting sufficient rest. It is also a smart thought to make time to unwind and to accomplish something that you need to do, instead of something that another person anticipates that you should do. You may track down that basic changes like this can have a colossal effect to your general viewpoint.

Take On Challenges

Individuals with low self-esteem frequently abstain from testing and difficult circumstances. One approach to improve your self-esteem can really be to take on a test. This doesn't imply that you need to do everything yourself—a piece of the test may be to look for help when you need it—however, be set up to take a stab at something that you realize will be difficult to accomplish.

By succeeding, you show yourself what you can accomplish.

The Importance of Small Steps

It is improbable that you will go from poor to great self-esteem for the time being.

You will likely discover you make little upgrades throughout some undefined time frame. The key is to investigate the long haul, as opposed to every day, and center around the 10,000-foot view, not the detail of how you felt at a specific second yesterday.

At the point when you feel better, or you accomplish something great, commend it—yet don't thrash yourself if you periodically slip once more into negative examples of reasoning. Simply get yourself again and attempt to think all the more decidedly. This will turn into a propensity in the long run, and you will find that your self-esteem has unobtrusively improved.

Enhance Social Skills

"Social abilities" is a lovely ambiguous term all alone. It covers a scope of circumstances and practices unreasonably immense to examine in one article.

When people say they need to improve their social abilities, I think what they truly mean is "I need to improve at conversing with strangers, make friends all the more effectively, and be more agreeable in friendly circumstances." So those are the themes I'll zero in on this guide (they're also the ones I have the most involvement in).

Here are some helpful methods to improve and build up your social abilities.

1. Try not to hide behind Your Phone

You can probably fault a portion of the issues you have with being social on the little PC you convey in your pocket. It's gotten satisfactory to take a gander at your telephone out in the open, and this has negatively affected social cooperation.

Before cells (particularly cell phones), you had basically no decision except to converse with individuals around you. Certainly, you could cover your face in a novel or notebook, yet both of these gadgets did not have the ease and simple access of a telephone.

These days, in any case, nearly everybody has their nose stuck in their telephone. And in light of the fact that it's gotten so socially adequate, it's not difficult to utilize your telephone to try not to cooperate with strangers (or even associates you'd prefer not to converse with).

If you need to associate with individuals, be that as it may, you need to take care of your telephone. It will appear to be abnormal from the start, possibly excruciating. However, if you need to have a discussion, you need to initially flag that you're available to talk.

Taking care of your telephone conveys a message that you need to talk, and it also makes you bound to take in your environmental factors (counting any potential discussion accomplices).

2. Accomplish More Things In Person

Nowadays, there are applications to convey everything from goods to toothpaste to tacos. Consolidate this with administrations that let you stream more media than you might devour in a lifetime, and it's not difficult to invest the majority of your energy inside, at home.

While these advanced administrations can help us set aside cash and time, they can also confine us from this present reality (and individuals who possess it). Without customary human contact, your social abilities can decay.

Hence, I urge you to accomplish more things face to face. Here are a couple of thoughts:

Shop for goods face to face rather than on the web.

Go out to eat as opposed to requesting conveyance (extra focuses if you welcome a friend or relative).

See a film at the auditorium as opposed to streaming it.

Buy books at a neighborhood book shop rather than on Amazon.

And the above are only a couple thoughts. You can most likely consider a lot more freedoms that identify with your interests and day by day exercises. The fact of the matter is to place yourself in contact with individuals (or possibly the potential for it).

3. Remove Your Headphones

I love earphones similarly as much as anyone else (likely more, taking into account how much music I tune in to). In any case, while earphones can be an incredible apparatus for liking the subtleties of a tune or zeroing in on significant work, they also disengage you from the world and others.

Wearing earphones says, "Kindly don't converse with me, I would prefer not to be annoyed." This is incredible when you don't need your collaborators to intrude on you, yet it's horrible when you need to interface with individuals. Similarly, as with your telephone, you need to show that you're available to talk if you need to have more discussions.

Taking care of the earphones (or taking out the AirPods) frees you up to more friendly cooperations. In addition, you'll notice new sonic subtleties like the melody of a specific bird or the murmur of different passing vehicles. Your experience of the world will be more extravagant generally speaking.

4. Discover Structured Social Activities

If you're a contemplative person, you may think that its difficult to start up discussions with random individuals in a bistro, bar, or line at the supermarket. This is because these circumstances are too open-finished, too ailing in structure. They put all the accentuation on talking, which can be abnormal and depleting when you're first gathering individuals.

To facilitate the pressing factor, I suggest discovering social exercises with structure. Thusly, you have another thing to do when you don't know what to say. Here are a couple of thoughts:

Board game evenings (numerous nearby breweries, coffeehouses, and public venues have these)

Sports classes

Church gatherings

Community band/symphony

Meetup gatherings (however make certain to pick one that is loner friendly)

In-individual classes (cooking, photography, painting, and so forth)

Craft gatherings (you can discover a great deal of these on Meetup)

The goal is to discover an action that offers you the chance to talk yet additionally another thing to zero in on when the discussion quiets.

5. Use "Open" Body Language

Non-verbal communication makes statements words never could. The manner in which an individual is standing or sitting, for example, can disclose to you a ton about how they're feeling. Understanding how to peruse these prompts (and how to utilize them) is critical to improving your social abilities.

At the point when you're attempting to be friendlier, you should utilize "open" non-verbal communication. Open non-verbal communication signs to others that you're keen on interfacing with them.

So what does this resemble by and by? Here are the key segments:

Uncross your legs and arms

Stand (or sit) upright

Turn towards individuals

Relax your shoulders (numerous individuals normally grip them)

Smile

If you do the above mentioned, you'll appear to be all the more friendly and "open" to conversing with individuals.

You can also utilize similar standards to check whether it's fitting to join a discussion. If individuals are standing/sitting with their bodies open (turned outward), then that can flag they're willing to have somebody join the discussion.

Then again, if two individuals are confronting one another and are by and large "stopped" from the remainder of the room, that is a sign they're having a closer to home or private discussion and don't need others to join.

Presently, having said the entirety of this, non-verbal communication isn't secure. You can't be 100% certain how somebody's inclination or if they need to converse with you. Unavoidably, there will be off-kilter minutes where you confound the circumstance. Which carries me to my next suggestion…

6. Embrace the Awkwardness

If you're putting forth an attempt to be more friendly, there will be off-kilter minutes. Regardless of whether it's going for a handshake when the other individual was endeavoring a clench hand knock, or simply the agony of not realizing what to say, ponderousness is difficult to stay away from.

Many individuals (myself included) put unnecessary focus on themselves to stay away from ungainliness. Since, in such a case that you're abnormal, that implies you've by one way or another flopped socially… correct? While this bodes well, it's a counterproductive conviction.

If you just spotlight on keeping away from clumsiness, then you'll rapidly abandon attempting to associate by any means.

And this is something contrary to what you need. So all things being equal, I propose you embrace the clumsiness. Rather than review abnormal minutes as a "disappointment," consider them to be an indication that you're stretching the boundaries of your usual range of familiarity.

Similarly, as with some other ability, you can just improve your social abilities with purposeful practice. And over the span of rehearsing, you will undoubtedly have a couple of off-kilter minutes. Regardless of whether you're the most outgoing, friendly individual in the world, you can't get away from cumbersomeness — it's simply a piece of being human.

7. Ask Questions

Keeping a discussion going with somebody you don't realize well can be difficult. So what are you expected to discuss? I can't respond to that, as each circumstance is different. Yet, I can offer you this piece of guidance: pose inquiries.

You've presumably heard the aphorism, "Individuals love to discuss themselves." Ask somebody about themselves, and they'll have no lack of comments.

The key, nonetheless, is to pose open-finished inquiries. That is, pose inquiries that don't have a basic "yes or no" reply.

It is the difference between Do you like living here? and What do you think about living here? Or then again the difference between Where did you grow up? and tell me about where you grew up (I understand that really isn't a "question," yet it really checks).

At the point when you pose open-finished inquiries, you set out the freedom for discourse. You study the individual you're conversing with, and that data fills in as fuel for additional discussion. Additionally, it removes a great deal of pressing factors from you.

8. Be a Good Listener

Posing open-finished inquiries is an extraordinary method to make a big difference for a discussion, however, be cautious. If you pose an excessive number of inquiries, you can appear to be mechanical or diverted. The exact opposite thing you need is for somebody to figure you're not tuning in to them.

In any case, how would you tune in? Viable listening is about something beyond latently accepting data. You need to show the other individual that you're tuning in. This comes from agreed articulations, non-verbal communication, and a healthy measure of quiet.

We should begin with insisting what the other individual is saying. For example, suppose somebody enlightens you concerning how they experienced childhood in a different country. In that case, you could say, That should give you a different point of view on the United States [or whatever nation you're right now in].

Offering confirmed expressions like these exhibits that you're occupied with the discussion and considering you're hearing.

Then, there's non-verbal communication. The accompanying non-verbal communication shows that you're tuning in:

Turning toward the individual (don't gaze vacantly at nothing in particular or turn away)

Nodding (or shaking your head)

Making eye to eye connection (simply be certain not to try too hard or it tends to be frightening)

At last, don't go on and on. Truly tune in; be calm and take in the thing the individual is saying.

9. Escape Your Head

It's not difficult to get so centered around the thing you will say next that you neglect to tune in and be available in the discussion. I actually battle with this, in any event, when conversing with dear friends. However, it's improved now that I'm aware of it.

Whenever you're having a discussion, check whether you discover yourself considering what you will say next instead of zeroing in on what the other individual is saying. You might be surprised how frequently it occurs.

By and large, monitoring this inclination is sufficient to improve it. However, if you're actually battling, I suggest attempting care reflection. This can help you control in your wandering psyche and spotlight more on the current second.

10. Try not to Force Humor

Being entertaining is an extraordinary method to make friends. Yet, not every person is clever. At any rate, not every person is amusing constantly. Not every person has that character. And that is OK. You don't need to be interesting to have discussions and construct extraordinary connections. There's room (and need) for genuine individuals on the planet too.

Whatever you do, don't attempt to constrain humor. Individuals can advise when you're attempting to be amusing. It's off-putting and awkward (except if you're doing some sort of nuanced stand-up daily schedule).

Simply act naturally. What you'll discover is that you'll unavoidably get a few chuckles simply over the span of talking.

11. Practice, Practice, Practice

The more effective social communications you have, the more certain you'll turn into. And as your certainty develops, mingling will get simpler (and even fun!). In any case, you can't construct your certainty if you're not getting out there and attempting.

This doesn't mean you need to go out to a different spot all week long. You can begin little, and you can in any case accept the alone time you need as a thoughtful person (indeed, you disregard it at your hazard).

To begin, track down an organized, agreeable action that allows you to rehearse your social abilities. Take a stab at applying the tips on this rundown. Then, develop to less natural social circumstances as your certainty increments.

Speak Confidently with Strangers

Meeting strangers is likely one of most people's greatest fears, close to talking before a group. Thankfully, it doesn't need to be as frightening an encounter as you would suspect. These ten simple tips will help you talk with a stranger easily.

Be set up to introduce contact

When you're at an occasion without assistance from any other person, don't believe that someone will come up and talk with you. People are called friendly individuals since they bob around and meet others. Standing in the corner believing someone will advance toward you won't go wherever. Try not to confound yourself and think this is a significant deal—introducing yourself is the solitary way you can meet someone else. Get out in the gathering and mix!

Go out alone

Don't generally go to occasions with a friend, significant other, or relative. Go alone, so you're compelled to meet others. If you go with somebody you're comfortable with, you're bound to remain and converse with the individual you definitely realize you can have discussions with. Also, no one can really tell who your partner will know. Imagine a scenario where a portion of their collaborators appear, and they leave you to go make proper acquaintance. You'll be left all alone in any case, so you need to prepare to be left all alone.

Try not to discuss about the weather

Nobody needs to stall out in an exhausting discussion. If you start with a cheesy conversation starter or a bland remark about the climate, don't be surprised when the other individual feigns exacerbation or leaves. Lines like those don't leave a lot of space to support socialization—they're more stand-alone proclamations than they are ice breakers. Moreover, it's ideal to avoid political or strict openers. Regardless of whether these points are in the information, no one can really tell what may annoy somebody. Stand by until you realize the individual to examine hard-hitting subjects. If you can't consider something fascinating all alone, simply start with a "Welcome, how are you?" and see where it goes from that point.

Encourage people to talk about themselves.

A considerable number of individuals' main subjects are—themselves! Whether or not you don't have a fascinating opener, you can, by and large, get some data about themselves, and they'll readily oblige you. Ask how they help a living, where they're from, or what they moved in school. If you get someone talking about their tendencies, you'll see their real characters come through. They'll be anxious to share their redirections, and you may find that you share something essentially!

But still share information about yourself.

Everybody likes to discuss themselves, however, they also prefer to find out about others. If you pose an excessive number of inquiries of another associate, they may feel like you're intrusive or giving them an exhaustive cross-examination. Besides, if you share a portion of your inclinations, that may trigger something they never thought to share. Who knew you both appreciated gathering stamps from South Africa?

Discover and talk about common interests.

Finding out about your new friend and sharing data about yourself should normally prompt tracking down some basic interests. Zero in on these and talk about them; no one can really tell when you'll discover some new information! At any rate, you could track down another friend to impart this leisure activity to. If you don't have any normal interests, don't stress! Few out of every odd stranger you meet is intended to turn into your new closest companion. You actually got this far in the discussion, so congratulate yourself!

Be friendly, not pushy or forceful.

Despite why you're attempting to meet new individuals, don't feel strain to obtain a pocketful of new friends. If you're terrified of disappointment or feel like you should meet another person, you'll seem to be forceful. If someone might not want to have a conversation with you, let them walk around without being pushy and endeavoring to stay close-lipped regarding them. Be laid back and go with the flow—it will make you have all the earmarks of being friendly, which suggests you'll have better conversations, and will undoubtedly have others approach you.

Try not to be humiliated if you're obviously apprehensive

If your voice breaks or your handshake is sweat-soaked, dismiss it. If you're a novice entertainer and can make it into a joke, call attention to it and get individuals giggling with you. If it's something that causes you to feel less sure, simply disregard it. Everybody gets apprehensive some of the time, so push past and proceed with the discussion. Try not to allow it to entangle you or humiliate you enough that you need to leave.

Let your personality shine through

Most importantly, act naturally. If you're making a decent attempt to engage everybody, you'll seem to be flakey and nobody will need to converse with you. It's an excess of work to be everything to everybody, so act naturally and, most importantly, live it up. Individuals will pay heed and be attracted to you.

Know when to end the conversation

Regardless of whether the discussion is a failure or a triumph, realize when to wrap it up. If you realize right off the bat that you would prefer not to continue to converse with somebody, track down a smooth, easy approach to proceed onward and meet another person. If you have a decent discussion and get along, tell your new friend that you need to leave, however, you'd love to get together again at some point. Get a telephone number or email address and leave the occasion high on your own prosperity!

The Conversation Skills

Conversations are supposed to be fun. They include individual associations between at least two individuals about something of interest. Be that as it may, numerous individuals stress over having a conversation. They are worried that they will not have the option to make a big difference in the conversation or what they will say.

Keeping communication going is something of an art, and one which a considerable lot of us presently appear to need. This portion clarifies how you can get familiar with this 'dying art' and have helpful and agreeable discussions with others.

The Rules of Conversation

1. The conversation is a Two-Way Street

The first and most significant standard of discussion is that it isn't about you, however, it's not about the other individual by the same token.

A discourse, one or the other way, isn't discussion. Attempt to accomplish harmony among talking and tuning in any discussion.

This is the place where online media makes life difficult. We're accustomed to broadcasting our perspectives and then reacting if others remark. That can feel like the start of a conversation yet when you're eye to eye, it's not aware to start by conveying your viewpoints.

All things being equal, have a go at posing an inquiry to build up shared belief. For instance: "What do you do?", or even "Isn't the climate beautiful?"

2. Be Polite and Friendly

Smiling, and being lovely, will take you far in conversational terms. Everyone would like to converse with someone friendly and beguiling. Regardless, what are the sensible segments of this?

3. Build affinity.

You can construct affinity by setting up some shared belief and by basically grinning and utilizing positive and supporting non-verbal communication. There is more about this on our page: Non-Verbal Communication.

4. Be pleasant.

Try not to express undesirable things about anybody. In light of everything, the individual you're talking about could be your new partner's dearest friend. And regardless of whether they're not, your new associate may not savor conversation about somebody despite their good faith (and neither should you). See our page on Friendliness for certain thoughts.

5. Try to keep away from antagonistic points on the first colleague.

It's fine to discuss administrative issues once you understand someone to some degree better. Right when you first meet someone, however, it's smarter to adhere to unbiased ground, which is why countless individuals talk about the climate. This is the place where 'casual conversation' comes in.

Anyway dull you discover somebody, it is best not to say as much!

Simply carry the discussion to an amenable close, maybe by saying something like "I should simply proceed to get this and that before they go. It's been truly ideal to visit you", or "Kindly pardon me, I vowed to assist with x and I see they need me now".

6. React to What They are Saying

To respond really to what someone has as of late said suggests that you need to tune in. You can't just mood killer and consider what you will say immediately. Regardless, if we're direct, by far most of us would surrender that we consistently do athat accurately

It's critical to zero in on the other individual, and what they're saying. You also need to consider their non-verbal communication.

If you think that its difficult to consider a remark, accordingly, take a stab at utilizing some 'filler' sentences, for example,

7. Use Gesturing to Help the Other Person

Right when a conversation is streaming commendably, it typically moves from one individual to the next. Nonetheless, if one or both are thinking that it's to a greater extent a battle to 'visit', you may think that it's accommodating to utilize 'motions toward' show the other individual that it is their chance to talk.

The most well-known kind of significant questions. These might be either open or shut.

Closed addresses welcome a yes/no answer.

In discussion, they may incorporate "Don't you concur?", and "Are you appreciating the gathering?" They are not actually welcoming the other individual to accomplish more than gesture and concur instead of sharing the discussion.

Open addresses welcome more data.

They open up the discussion to the next individual and welcome them to take part. Therefore, in the discussion, they are regularly called 'solicitations'. Open inquiries regularly start 'How… ?' or 'Why… .?'

8. Make Emotional Connections

Obviously, it is totally conceivable to direct a discussion altogether at the degree of casual chitchat, with nothing significant being said.

Yet, the discussion is also an approach to investigate whether you wish to know somebody better and construct a relationship with them. It can subsequently be helpful to understand how to utilize discussion to make and fabricate emotional associations.

9. The Importance of Self-Confidence

Self-confidence is one's capacity to pass judgment on his own social and individual standing as for his current circumstance and have the option to determine fulfillment out of it.

Self-confidence is affected by factors like childhood, workplace, and levels of commitment towards seeking after a reason. High self-certainty is a significant factor in improving business ties and adjusting individual life.

There is a renowned saying that when you start the trip of your master life, have confidence in your abilities. Since you have not exhibited your abilities yet.

Directly from the early occasions through the development of the human culture, this colloquialism couldn't be more genuine with regards to the present. These are incredibly serious occasions that we are living in, and self-certainty is perhaps the greatest mainstay of solidarity and self-food for an individual, more so now than any other time in recent memory.

Why Need Confidence?

Being sure about your qualities assists you in withdrawing boldness and goals when hard times arise in life. It assists you with keeping things in context and back yourself when every other person says that the assignment ahead is almost difficult to finish in the specified time.

A sure individual has sufficient capacity to understand his limits and realizes how to compensate for that with his determination and qualities.

Since we have perceived how self-confidence depends upon your obvious ability to manage movement, how about we examine the activities that help to develop a self-appreciation certainty.

Actions That Help Cultivating Sense Of Self-Confidence.

Self-confidence flourishes in an air where the individual is given helpful input and the emphasis are consistently on the positive.

In a particularly working climate, a certain individual will actually want to rehearse his abilities and ability past assumptions, as he will get a chance to define goals, fail to remember his own previous slip-ups, and learn new things.

Then again, an individual's self-confidence can be truly hampered in a climate where there is a consistent examination with others and where assumptions are ridiculous. Persons are set in disagreement to one another according to their exhibition in the numbers game.

In these conditions, an individual will be compelled to support a serious unhealthys attitude by falling back on out of line implies for progress, tuning in to disgraceful good examples, being too unforgiving in making a decision about his own exhibitions, and disparaging his own capacities.

Such a climate breeds an unhealthy working environment where the pressure is more on beating each other's exhibitions than meeting up collectively to aid each other. Such associations may top for a long time, notwithstanding, they ultimately crash.

Individuals with High Self-Confidence

Individuals with high self-confidence approach their issues differently when contrasted with others. They know the significance of building connections and thus, they love meeting new individuals to get and share groundbreaking thoughts. This nature of theirs makes them amiable, as they are continually able to be in a discussion that gives equivalent significance and regard to each of the individuals who have taken part in it.

Sure individuals love communicating their thoughts before others, as they are emotionally secure enough to take productive reactions and reject emotional ones. That doesn't imply that they are egotistical; unexpectedly, they offer everybody the chance to put their focuses forward. Notwithstanding, they dare to adhere to their choice despite a ton of resistance to their thoughts, if they are persuaded what they are doing is correct.

There are two results to any choice taken – it is possible that it ends up being the right one, or you fall flat. Notwithstanding, what separates a sure individual is that he doesn't supervisor around on naysayers when he succeeds.

Moreover, a self-sure individual has the modesty to recognize his slip-ups and gain from them when he falls flat. This targeted approach towards both achievement and disappointment is the thing that makes a certain individual an adorable and decent character.

Individuals with Low Self-Confidence

When contrasted with individuals with high self-certainty, individuals with low self-certainty have a brutal and basic perspective on themselves. They are inclined to taking emotional choices, rather than speculation judiciously. They will in general be in their "caverns" rather than meeting new individuals. They attempt to evade new organizations and try not to meet new individuals.

An under-certain individual will in general feel that he has nothing considerable or valuable to add to any interaction. This sensation of low self-worth joined with a total disavowal towards any change makes an under-sure individual incredibly susceptive to abuse and undervaluation.

Individuals with low confidence falter in imparting their contemplations and insights, as they might suspect their perspectives will be derided in broad daylight. What's more, their previous encounters and connections with individuals have not effectively improved their self-worth and change their perspectives about their profitability and significance.

This is the place where beneficial air comes into play. Each individual gains from his environmental factors and your self-confidence rely straightforwardly upon the sort of individuals you meet and the kind of conversations you have with them. While self-sure individuals associate with individuals whom they have something to gain from, certain individuals are persuaded that they can't change and will be underestimated disregarding what they do.

Here are the advantages of greater self-confidence:

Being your best under pressure. Competitors, performers, and entertainers will verify the signature of an undeniable degree of certainty. At the point when you're sure, you perform up to your latent capacity and you need to play out your best when it tallies the most, when under tension.

Influencing others. Self-confident individuals frequently impact others all the more promptly. This aide when selling a thought or item or haggling at work or home.

Having authority and chief presence. Self-certainty has a major influence on administration and leadership presence. You make such a presence by how you think, act (counting how you convey your body), and utilize your voice.

Exuding a more inspirational mentality. At the point when you feel sure about yourself, you trust you have a significant and significant spot on the planet, giving you an inspirational demeanor.

Feeling valued. At the point when you're confident, you understand what you dominate at and that you have esteem.

Rising to the top. Searching for a promotion? The more confidence you have, the more probable you are to be advanced.

Reducing negative contemplations. More noteworthy self-confident permits you to encounter independence from self-uncertainty and negative contemplations about yourself.

Experiencing more fearlessness and less tension. More noteworthy certainty makes you more willing to face savvy challenges and more ready to move outside your usual range of familiarity.

Having more prominent independence from social tension. Turning out to be happier with acting naturally diminishes worry about others' opinions about you. How freeing!

Energy and inspiration to make a move. Confidence gives you sure energy to make a move to accomplish your own and expert goals and dreams. The more exceptionally energetic and stimulated you are, the almost certain you are to make a quick move.

Being more joyful. Confident individuals will in general be more joyful and happier with their lives than individuals who need self-certainty.

Love Your Self

A considerable lot of the world's generally beautiful and notable individuals furtively need self-love. VIPs are an incredible illustration of this. They appear to be so great and numerous individuals need to be actually similar to them. In any case, they fight similar fears and nerves as we do. A great many fans who appreciate and regard you won't bring happiness. Just self-love will do that.

Notwithstanding, if happiness isn't found through outer methods, where then do we start?

To authentically look for happiness, we should return to the quest for inward self-love. Valid and authentic happiness can't start except if it comes from love. Moreover, love can't happen except if we first love ourselves.

Here are the ways to love yourself!

Use Daily Affirmations

We should begin with affirmations. Affirmations are, basically, self-offered praises. Others may laud us, yet to fabricate authentic self-love we need to figure out how to self-acclaim. Affirmations assist us with recognizing our own gifts, without depending on others to show us. Having the option to accept our qualities and goodness, without the endorsement of others, is simply the initial step to fearless love.

If you've battled with self-love before, figuring out how to love yourself once more or love yourself interestingly can feel overpowering and scary. Affirmations are a delicate and astounding prologue to authentic self-love. Affirmations work to help support your self-regard, which thusly, adds to that goal of fearless self-love.

Stop Your Negative Self Talk

Going hand in hand with affirmations is the act of thought halting, and specifically, attempting to cease negative self-talk. Regularly we are the cause of all our own problems. We can be held detainee as far as we could tell, yet fail to remember that we can break free whenever given the inspiration and instruments to do as such.

Our contemplations can take us in numerous ways, both great and awful. For some, it feels regular and simple to accept the most exceedingly awful, over-examine, make a quick judgment call, or even catastrophize. These reasoning blunders are a snare for tension and low self-regard, yet additionally an unavoidable reason for minimal self-love and unhappiness.

Travel Alone

Perhaps the most ideal approach to change your life's latent capacity is to travel alone.

It can break you liberated from your usual range of familiarity, increment your confidence, and further build up your instinct.

In one investigation, numerous members conceded having friends that could go with them on a get-away, at the same time, they decided to travel solo for individual reasons. Their reasons were; self-disclosure, self-awareness, courage, and meeting new individuals.

Travel Once A Year

This may be thoroughly out of your typical scope of commonality, yet that is something to be thankful for! If you can go in isolation, this will be an exceptional self-love understanding. You will learn new things about yourself just as another culture. This also helps with conveying you by and by from your standard regular practice.

Pardon Yourself for Your Mistakes

Thinking about your errors can assist you with excusing and neglect. If you can glance back at some helpless decisions you may have made, and pardon yourself, you can begin to proceed onward and disregard the past. Adoring yourself in spite of any errors you made in the past is incredible for your self-worth.

Surprise Yourself

Offer things a chance of your control, and say yes to things you would not routinely say yes to. This will also help you with getting more familiar with yourself. You may find that you like things you never recognized or endeavored. Endeavor to get away from your standard scope of commonality and see what happens (it will surely be positive!).

Start a Journal

If you can record your musings and emotions, you can return sometime in the not too distant future and perceive how you adapted to specific circumstances.

This is also a good way for you to dispose of any negative encounters and emotions, assisting you with zeroing in on the beneficial things and gaining from the awful.

Offer Yourself A Break

We can be no picnic for ourselves once in a while, it's characteristic, however you need to offer yourself a reprieve occasionally.

Nobody is great, and you can't anticipate that you should be so.

Several things happen yet you need to recognize them and not be too hard on yourself.

Figure out How to Love Yourself by Saying No to Others

Now and again we do a great deal for people, we like to fulfill others, so we will overall stretch ourselves exorbitantly dainty and spotlight on all that we can. We can disregard to really focus on ourselves sometimes, so that is why it is adequate to say no. Focus on yourself when you can, or if you are overwhelmed.

Make a List Of Your Accomplishments

Causing a once-over of what you to have achieved is an unfathomable strategy to fall wildly enamored for yourself. This makes you have an inspirational attitude toward yourself and find happiness from what you have achieved. You can once in a while center on the negatives and disregard the positives, so this is an extraordinary method to help yourself to remember what you have accomplished.

Seek after New Interests

It's incredible to take a stab at something new that you have needed to go after some time or have been too frightened to even consider doing.

No one can really tell what you may appreciate until you attempt it, so think about another leisure activity you could attempt, or go to a spot you've needed to go to for some time.

Give Yourself Credit Where Credit Is Due

Commend your accomplishments! Very much like when you list your achievements, it's acceptable to really praise your accomplishments. Enlighten others concerning what you have done, share your experience and be pleased with what you have done. Give yourself the credit you merit.

Work On Your Self-Trust

An incredible method to show yourself self-love is to confide in yourself and your own impulses. You are in all likelihood going to realize what is best for you, and self-trust is a stage to self-love. You need to trust yourself before you can trust in others, so check out your gut and trust how you feel.

Deal with Yourself

This one most likely appears glaringly evident, yet dealing with yourself has a major influence in figuring out how to love yourself, and many individuals don't do it. If you manage yourself, you will be basically the best structure. Explore our self-care musings to kick you off.

You could utilize the Law of Attraction to begin running after the life you need to live, which incorporates adoring yourself.

10. Charismatic Public Speaker

Regardless of whether we're talking in a group meeting or introducing ourselves before a crowd of people, we as a whole need to talk openly every now and then.

We can do this seriously, and the result emphatically influences the way that individuals consider us. This is the reason public talking causes such a lot of uneasiness and concern.

Fortunately, with intensive readiness and practice, you can conquer your anxiety and perform astoundingly well. This article and video clarify how.

The Importance of Public Speaking

Regardless of whether you don't have to make standard introductions before a gathering, there are a lot of circumstances where great public talking abilities can help you advance your profession and set out open doors.

For example, you might need to discuss your association at a gathering, deliver a discourse subsequent to tolerating an honor, or show a class to newcomers. Addressing a crowd of people also incorporates online introductions or talks; for example, when preparing a virtual group, or when addressing a gathering of clients in an internet meeting.

Great public talking abilities are significant in different parts of your life, too. You may be approached to deliver a discourse at a friend's wedding, give a commendation for a loved one, or move a gathering of volunteers at a cause occasion.

To put it plainly, being a decent open speaker can upgrade your standing, support your self-confidence, and open up incalculable freedoms.

Be that as it may, while great abilities can open entryways, helpless ones can close them. For instance, your supervisor may rule against advancing you subsequent to enduring a severely conveyed introduction. You may lose a significant new agreement by neglecting to interface with a plausibility during an endeavor to sell something. Or then and there again you could set up a vulnerable association with your new gathering, since you stagger over your words and don't take a gander at people without jumping.

Guarantee that you sort out some way to talk well!

Strategies for Becoming a Better Speaker

Fortunately talking out in the open is a learnable ability. In that capacity, you can utilize the accompanying methodologies to improve as a speaker and moderator.

Plan Appropriately

In the first place, make sure that you plan your correspondence suitably. When you do this, consider how significant a book's first passage is; if it doesn't get you, you're probably going to put it down. A similar guideline goes for your discourse: all along, you need to interest your crowd.

For instance, you could begin with a fascinating measurement, feature, or reality that relates to what in particular you're discussing and reverberates with your crowd.

Arranging also assists you with thinking and reacting quickly. This is predominantly important for unusual inquiry and answer meetings or a minute ago correspondences.

Practice

There's a valid justification that we say, "Careful discipline brings about promising results!" You essentially can't be a confident, convincing speaker without training.

To get practice, look for freedoms to talk before others. For instance, Toastmasters is a club equipped specifically towards trying speakers, and you can get a lot of training at Toastmasters meetings. You could also place yourself in circumstances that require public talking, for example, by broadly educating a gathering from another division, or by electing to talk at group gatherings.

If you will convey an introduction or arranged discourse, make it as ahead of schedule as could be expected. The prior you set up it, the extra time you will need to practice.

Practice it a lot of times alone, using the resources you'll rely upon at the event, and, as you practice, change your words until they stream effectively and with no issue.

Then, if fitting, do a spurious spat front of a little crowd: this will help you quiet your butterflies and cause you to feel better with the material. Your crowd can also give you helpful criticism, both on your material and on your presentation.

Engage With Your Audience

At the point when you talk, attempt to draw in your crowd. This causes you to feel less secluded as a speaker and keeps everybody engaged with your message. If suitable, pose driving inquiries focused to people or gatherings, and urge individuals to take an interest and pose inquiries.

Remember that a couple of words decline your power as a speaker. For instance, consider how these sentences sound: "I essentially need to add that I figure we can meet these goals" or "I basically think this plan is a respectable one." The words "just" and "I think" limit your force and conviction. Do whatever it takes not to use them.

A tantamount word is "truly," as in, "Truly, I'd like to add that we were underspending last quarter." When you use "truly," it passes on a sensation of convenience or even surprises. In light of everything, say what things are. "We were underspending last quarter" is clear and direct.

Also, center around how you're talking. If you're uneasy, you may talk quickly. This expands the chances that you'll stagger over your words or say something you don't mean. Force yourself to ease off by breathing significantly. Try not to be hesitant to amass your contemplations; stops are a significant piece of the conversation, and they make you sound confident, normal, and authentic.

At last, try not to peruse in exactly the same words from your notes. All things considered, make a rundown of significant focuses on prompt cards, or, as you improve at public talking, attempt to remember what you will say – you can in any case allude back to your sign cards when you need them.

Pay Attention to Body Language

If you're unaware of it, your non-verbal communication will give your crowd consistent, unobtrusive signs about your inward state. If you're apprehensive or don't have faith in what you're saying, the crowd can before long know.

Concentrate on your non-verbal correspondence: stand upstanding, take full breaths, take a gander at people without wincing, and smile. Do whatever it takes not to slant toward one leg or use flags that vibe unnatural.

Many people like to talk behind a platform when giving their introductions. While platforms can be helpful for holding notes, they put a boundary between you and the crowd. They can also turn into a "brace," giving you a concealing spot from the handfuls or many eyes that are on you.

Rather than standing behind a platform, stroll around and use motions to connect with the crowd. This development and energy will also come through in your voice, making it more dynamic and energetic.

Think Positively

Good reasoning can have an immense effect on the achievement of your correspondence since it assists you with feeling more confident.

Fear makes it very simple to slip into a pattern of negative self-talk, particularly just before you talk, while self-undermining contemplations, for example, "I'll never be acceptable at this!" or "I will fail miserably!" bring down your confidence and increment the odds that you will not accomplish what you're really prepared to do.

Use affirmations and representation to raise your confidence. This is particularly significant just before your dissertation or introduction. Picture giving an effective introduction, and imagine how you will feel once it's finished and when you've had a constructive outcome for other people. Utilize positive affirmations, for example, "I'm appreciative I have the chance to help my crowd" or "I will progress admirably!"

Cope With Nerves

How frequently have you tuned in to or watched a speaker who truly wrecked? Chances are, the appropriate response is "not regularly."

At the point when we need to talk before others, we can imagine horrible things occurring. We envision neglecting each point we need to make, dropping from our apprehension, or doing so terribly that we'll lose our business. In any case, those things won't ever occur! We create them in our minds and end up more restless than we should be.

Numerous individuals refer to addressing a crowd of people as their greatest fear, and a fear of disappointment is frequently at the base of this. Public talking can lead your "battle or flight" reaction to kick in: adrenaline flows through your circulation system, your pulse expands, you sweat, and your breath turns out to be quick and shallow.

Albeit these indications can be irritating or in any event, crippling, the Inverted-U Model shows that a specific measure of pressing factor improves execution. By changing your mentality, you can utilize apprehensive energy for your potential benefit.

In the first place, put forth an attempt to quit pondering yourself, your apprehension, and your fear. All things being equal, center on your crowd: what you're not kidding "about them." Remember that you're attempting to help or instruct them somehow or another, and your message is a higher priority than your fear. Focus on the crowd's needs and needs, rather than your own.

If time permits, utilize profound breathing activities to moderate your pulse and give your body the oxygen it needs to perform. This is particularly significant just before you talk.

Take full breaths from your gut, hold everyone for a few seconds, and let it out gradually.

Groups are scarier than people, so consider your discourse a discussion that you're having with one individual. Despite the fact that your crowd might be 100 individuals, center around each friendly face in turn, and converse with that individual as though the person is the just one in the room.

Watch Recordings of Your Speeches

Whenever possible, record your introductions and talks. You can improve your talking abilities significantly by watching yourself later, and then dealing with improving in regions that turned out poorly.

As you watch, notice any verbal eases back down, for instance, "um" or "like." Look at your non-verbal correspondence: would you say you are impacting, slanting toward the stage, or slanting overwhelmingly on one leg? This is safe to say that you are looking at the group? Did you smile? Did you talk evidently reliably?

Focus on your emotions. Do they seem regular or constrained? Ensure that individuals can see them, particularly if you're standing behind a platform.

Last, take at how you handled interferences, for example, a sniffle or an inquiry that you weren't ready for. Does your face show surprise, delay, or inconvenience? If thus, work on overseeing interferences like these easily, so that you're shockingly better sometime later.

11. The Personality Types

What makes someone what their character is? Each individual has their own personal idea character type — if they are effervescent or saved, delicate or tough. Therapists who attempt to coax out the study of our identity are characterized by individual differences in how individuals will think, feel, and carry on.

There are numerous approaches to assess character, however, analysts have for the most part abandoned attempting to isolate mankind flawlessly into types. All things being equal, they center on character attributes.

The most generally acknowledged of these characteristics are the Big Five:

- Openness

- Conscientiousness
- Extraversion
- Agreeableness
- Neuroticism

The Big 5 are the ingredients that make up every person's character. An individual may have a scramble of transparency, a ton of scruples, a normal measure of extraversion, a lot of appropriateness, and practically no neuroticism by any means. Or on the other hand, someone could be offensive, masochist, contemplative, faithful, and barely open by any means. This is what every attribute involves:

Openness

Openness is shorthand for "Openness to encounter." People who are high in transparency appreciate the experience. They're interested and like craftsmanship, a creative mind, and new things. The saying of the open individual maybe."

Individuals low in transparency are the exact inverse: They like to adhere to their propensities, stay away from new encounters, and presumably aren't the most daring eaters. Changing character is normally viewed as an intense interaction, yet transparency is a character attribute that has been established to be responsible to change in adulthood. In a recent report, individuals who took psilocybin, or psychedelic "sorcery mushrooms," turned out to be more open after the experience. The impact endured in any event a year, proposing that it very well may be perpetual.

Discussing trial drug use, California's take a stab at anything society is no legend. An investigation of character attributes across the United States delivered in 2013 found that receptiveness is generally pervasive on the West Coast.

Conscientiousness

Individuals who are honest are coordinated and have a solid feeling of obligation. They're trustworthy, trained, and accomplishment-centered. You will not discover scrupulous sorts streaming off on round-the-world excursions with just a rucksack; they're organizers.

Individuals low in conscientiousness are more unconstrained and freewheeling. They may incline toward thoughtlessness. Conscientiousness is a useful quality to have, as it has been connected to accomplishment in school and at work.

Extraversion

Extraversion versus contemplation is potentially the most unmistakable character characteristic of the Big Five. The greater amount of an extravert somebody is, the, even more, a people person they are. Extraverts are loquacious, amiable, and draw energy from swarms. They will in general be decisive and happy in their social associations.

Recluses, then again, need a lot of alone time, maybe on the grounds that their cerebrums cycle social communication differently. Inner-directedness is frequently mistaken for bashfulness, yet the two aren't something similar. Bashfulness suggests a fear of social communications or powerlessness to work socially. Thoughtful people can be totally beguiling at parties — they simply lean toward solo or little gathering exercises

Agreeableness

Agreeableness estimates the degree of an individual's glow and thoughtfulness. The more pleasant somebody is, the almost certain they are to be trusted, useful, and empathetic. Revolting individuals are cold and doubtful of others, and they're more averse to participate.

Men who are high in pleasantness are decided to be better artists by ladies, proposing that body development can flag character. (Scruples also make for great artists, as indicated by a similar 2011 investigation.) But in the work environment, offensive men really procure more than pleasant folks. Unsavory ladies didn't show a similar compensation advantage, recommending that a straightforward attitude is remarkably helpful to men.

Being jealous, which can prompt individuals to be seen as not pleasing, was discovered to be the most widely recognized character type out of the four examinations by a report distributed in August 2016 in the diary Science Advances. Jealous individuals feel undermined when another person is more fruitful than they are.

Neuroticism

To understand neuroticism, look no farther than George Costanza of the long-running sitcom "Seinfeld." George is acclaimed for his despondencies, which show liabilities on his broken godparents. He worries about everything, focuses on germs and contamination, and once leaves a position of work since his anxiety over not looming a private bathroom is unnecessarily overwhelming.

George may be a high on the neuroticism scale, though, the character quality is genuine. Individuals high in neuroticism stress oftentimes and effectively slip into nervousness and sorrow. If everything is working out positively, masochist individuals will in general discover things to stress over. One 2012 investigation found that when psychotic individuals with great pay rates acquired raises, the additional pay really made them less cheerful.

Fascinatingly, people who are low in neuroticism will in general be emotionally stable and well-adjusted.

Obviously, neuroticism is associated with a lot of awful wellbeing results. Masochist individuals pass on more youthful than the emotionally steady, potentially on the grounds that they go to tobacco and liquor to facilitate their nerves.

However, potentially the creepiest reality about neuroticism is that parasites can cause you to feel that way. And we're not discussing the normal nervousness that may accompany realizing that a tapeworm has made a home in your gut. Undetected disease by the parasite Toxoplasma gondii may make individuals more inclined to neuroticism, a recent report found.

12. Do It and Boost Your Social

Influence

Never again is your social significance assessed solely by the number of enthusiasts you have. More significant than sum is the idea of responsibility you have with people who follow you. Resources measure this level of responsibility as a way to deal with quantifying your effect. The social effect is the effect you have on others' emotions, estimations, and practices. Perhaps the most outstanding influencer is Oprah. She can recommend a book or thing, and rapidly her aficionados are buying.

Impact is significant for a few reasons. Directors need impact to empower individuals who work with them to complete things. Bloggers compete for impact to get supports. At last, the advantage of social impact in your private company is that it can isolate yourself as a trained professional and pioneer. Here some things you can do to secure social effect.

1. Give worth. The more you give, the more you'll get, therefore. A couple of gathering like to grasp their best stuff to sell in their business. Nonetheless, don't be hesitant to give your allies important, obliging tips that will benefit them. The more worth you give, the more your lovers will attract and tell others.

2. Offer the love. While you should share your own business considerations and tips, sharing information from different resources will show that you center around your industry and give your allies the best information to pay little notice to the source. People whose information you share will regularly offer back in kind.

3. Draw in with influencers. Do whatever it takes not to follow or comment with the top experts in your field basically for the goal of getting them to recommend you or pull you up to their level. Remember, sway is obtained. Take everything into account, partner, offer, and discuss information and considerations with others in your industry. Exactly when they see you hear what you're saying or feel you have something of significant worth to share, they'll attract you also.

4. Tap into feeling. Influencers every now and again have evangelist disciples, not in the exacting sense, yet rather as in these people believe in and are amped up for the influencer.

Building an associated with stimulated after requires exploiting emotions, whether or not it's sharing lively, engaging, or even angry information, regardless of the way that be careful about being negative consistently.

5. Be pleasing. The effect is about people checking out you, and the best way to that is to listen to them. Zero in on their prerequisites, which will allow you to pass on regard. Respond to and attract them. Fans that vibe heard will undoubtedly attract with you and offer your information to others, in this way expanding your effect.

Social impact is something most money managers need, yet it's not got basically through tweeting at the correct occasions of day or purchasing the most supporters. Impacted is procured, gradually, through authentic sharing of data, tips and different things important to devotees. It develops gradually, however if done right, is solid, and turns into an amazing power in developing your business.

Conclusion

Social skills are important because they are the main key to success that such countless youngsters need in their lives. Numerous individuals battle identifying with their companions and having positive associations since they have never figured out how or in light of the fact that they experience issues summing up across different social circumstances. People learn how to successfully apply social skills through cognitive and behavioral approaches. Conduct approaches are utilized to unequivocally show an ability and psychological methodologies, for example, critical thinking, assist people with applying the abilities in intricate and conflicting circumstances. Social expertise preparing can be concentrated, in a treatment peer gathering, or it tends to be joined consistently all through the day, as genuine world, authentic circumstances introduce themselves.

CPSIA information can be obtained
at www.ICGtesting.com
Printed in the USA
BVHW041203080621
609008BV00005B/1351

9 781802 710250